Black Male Violence in Perspective

Black Male Violence in Perspective

Toward Afrocentric Intervention

P. Tony Jackson

LEXINGTON BOOKS
Lanham • Boulder • New York • London

Published by Lexington Books
An imprint of The Rowman & Littlefield Publishing Group, Inc.
4501 Forbes Boulevard, Suite 200, Lanham, Maryland 20706
www.rowman.com

Unit A, Whitacre Mews, 26-34 Stannary Street, London SE11 4AB

British Library Cataloguing in Publication Information Available

Library of Congress Cataloging-in-Publication Data

Jackson, P. Tony, 1959-
Black male violence in perspective : toward Afrocentric intervention / P. Tony Jackson.
p. cm.
Includes bibliographical references and index.
ISBN 978-0-7391-9163-7 (cloth : alk. paper) -- ISBN 978-0-7391-9164-4 (electronic)
1. African American men--Psychology. 2. Aggressiveness--Cross-cultural studies. 3. Violence--
Cross-cultural studies. 4. Cultural psychiatry. 5. Ethnopsychology. I. Title.
RC451.5.N4J33 2015
616.85'8200896073--dc23

2015003543

Printed in the United States of America

Contents

Contents

List of Figures and Tables

Foreword

Many have noted that the psychological effects the ideology of white supremacy and European imperialism, in the form of slavery and colonialism, has had on Africa and her people have never been fully addressed and understood. However, the development of the academic discipline and professional practice of Black psychology has changed the intellectual landscape, and Dr. Tony Jackson's text, *Black Male Violence in Perspective: Towards Afrocentric Intervention* is a welcomed contribution to our geography of knowing.

In Black psychology, Sakhu Sheti/Djaer has been offered as a penetrating search, study, and understanding that requires an investigative approach that always seeks the deeper meaning of phenomena and explores every aspect of reality. The notion of Sakhu Sheti/Djaer, in effect, requires a deep, profound, and penetrating search, study, and understanding of the African-American (Black) experience by (1) clarifying our definition, meaning, and resolute position/purpose in the world, (2) analyzing and describing the concrete human conditions which affect and influence our collective human development and consciousness, (3) prescribe and excite solutions and actions, that will free African people from both material and spiritual degradation.[1]

Dr. Jackson provides a detailed analysis of the problem of violence, especially relative to Black men, and unpacks the statistics in such a unique way that the humanity of Black men, as the pain behind the data, is not replaced with statistical reality making. In exploring the historical context of violence, Tony reveals the deeper meaning of violence and locates the meaning of Blackness and Maleness as target-created pathology through the nature of American society and its major tool of indoctrination, media technology. With this clarity, the reader is taken on a journey that provides insight into the consequence of violence against Black men, i.e., the three-headed dragon of frustration, depression and anger and attempts at its prevention, intervention and healing.

Dr. Jackson is at his best when he responds to the call to "improve violence prevention programming for young African-American males." In building on Diop's profound observation that "imperialism, which people of color all around the world have suffered under, is likened to a pre-historic hunter who first kills spiritually and culturally before killing physically," Tony accepts the charge to restore wellness by adding to the African-centered framework developed, in part, by Nobles, Akbar, Wright, Azibo, White, Meyers, Parham and Kambon, who have with different intensity called for the restoration of the African spirit. Grounded in ancient Kemetic frameworks and traditional BaKongo episteme, this book "pierces the paradigm" of European hegemony and allows the Black Psychology practitioner the opportunity to participate in the "reciprocal rebirthing" of our wellness and wholeness.

While ending with an anatomy of a study of real world attempts to change violence outcomes, Dr. Jackson's work has greater value than the testing of hypotheses concerning the inclusion of culturally relevant, socio-historically based materials in mainstream therapies that prove or disprove their efficaciousness for young African-American men. The value of this book is that the reading of it helps to prescribe and excite solutions and actions, which will help free African people, especially Black men, from both material and spiritual degradation brought about by violence. In light of the constant killing of Black men (by white law enforcement officers) that has currently ignited a national "Black Lives Matter" movement drawing international attention, this book is both timely and highly significant.

Black Male Violence in Perspective: Towards Afrocentric Intervention is more than a must-read. It is a work that must be studied and must be applied because, in the tradition of the Sakhu Shetist/Djaer, Dr. Tony Jackson provides us with a description, prescription, and justification for the effective use of an African-centered restoration project.

Wade W. Nobles, PhD

Ifagbemi Sangodare, Nana Kwaku Berko, I, Bejana, Onebunne
Co-founder, the Association of Black Psychologists
Professor Emeritus, Africana Studies and Black Psychology, SFSU
Executive Director, The Institute for the Advanced Study of Black Family
     Life & Culture

NOTE

1. Nobles, W. W. "Fundamental Task and Challenge of Black Psychology" in The Journal of Black Psychology Vol 39(3), June 2013, p292-256

Preface

This book is not for everyone. But if you are serious about understanding how the dynamics of "race" and fear drive the socio-political and economic forces that converge to shape the lives of African-descended youth in general and particularly of African-descended young men in America, then this book is for you. If you are truly interested in moving towards meaningful solutions to the violence that plagues too many of our communities and are not afraid to face the current and historic role American society has played in creating and maintaining the violence it purports to abhor, this book is for you. I do not attempt to pull punches, for the situation is too dire. Black men are dying and many of us are transitioned, in droves, into a system that can only be described as chattel slavery. There is no time (nor intention) to take care of "white folk" in this analysis. Many in this society are finally catching up to where we, as Black psychologists, have been for quite some time…that is…that racism is, in fact, a mental disease/disorder which represents internally and externally, consciously and unconsciously…that it is ultimately fear-based and interwoven into the deep cultural structure of European society, and that "sick" people create "sick" institutions. The miscarriage of justice in Ferguson, Missouri, exemplified by the utilization of "witness #40" in a secret and highly biased legal process euphemistically called "grand jury," stands as evidence of a system designed for obfuscation yet hypocritically referred to as a "justice" system. In this time of increased awareness of state sanctioned murder of young Black men and women, even corporate media outlets are asking the question, "Is it time to have a new discussion on race?" as if there exists some previous discussion they *can* point too.

Finally, we as human beings are enlivened by spirit, imbued with the potential to reach heights unimaginable. "Isms", including racism, erodes this potential, destroying opportunities for growth and development for both victims and perpetrators. To use Domestic Violence as an example, in this country, thankfully, the dialogue has moved away from blaming the victim in domestic violence cases. Perhaps through this work, the reader can garner support and insight in their effort towards moving away from blaming the victims of racism and community terrorism as well as generate new and robust programs to immunize, strengthen and enliven our youth to withstand the vagaries of racism in this society at every level and reach their potential.

Acknowledgments

"Yesterday is History, Today is a Miracle, Tomorrow is a Mystery. History is the Key to unlocking the Mystery of the Miracle."

I have borrowed this phrase from one of the major mentors in my life and career, Dr. Wade Nobles (Nana Kwaku Berko I, Ifagbemi Sangodare, Bejana). I will forever be indebted to him and the group of fifty-eight psychologists and students who in 1968 took the bold and unprecedented action of walking out of the APA in protest and establishing what would become the Association of Black Psychologists. They represented a group of individuals who were willing to risk their careers (and some, their status) to deal with the lack of methodology for addressing issues children like me were facing and would face in time, long before I was ever aware of their presence.

I am thankful to the ancestors, Franz Fanon, Cheik Ante Diop, Fu Kia, Asa Hilliard, John Jackson, John Henrik-Clark, Hon. Elijah Muhammad, Amos Wilson, Ivan Van Sertima, Chancellor Williams, Bobby Wright, Reginald Jones, and a host of others who laid the groundwork for the reclamation of factual history and shook the foundations of mainstream historical perspective. I am forever grateful for Drs. Naim Akbar, Nobles, Kambon, Bob Williams, Reggie White, Parham, Cress-Welsing, Azibo, James-Meyers, Goddard as well as Randall Robinson and a host of giants in the field who have provided a basis for scholarly analysis of our condition.

When I think about the ten-plus years' process of writing this book, I reflect on the many times I would pick up the writing of it only to set it down in the face of whatever the *crisis-de-jour* might be (and there were many). My work places me in contact with many students and unfortunately, the benefits of the job go along with the challenges of having to say goodbye to promising students whose lives are cut down far too early in their journey. To the Marcel Angelo Johnsons and Royal Bernsteins, I say thank you, for your unfortunate tragedies helped me pick this work back up.

As I have journeyed with the Oscar Grant Foundation and joined Oscar's Uncle Bobby and his Aunt Beatrice in their honorable work through the Love Not Blood Campaign, I thank them for their friendship and for helping re-ignite the passion for completing this work. To Oscar Grant, Trayvon Martin, Eric Garner, Kendrick Johnson, Latasha Harlings, Alan Blueford, Amidou Diallo, Sean Bell, Jordan Davis, Renisha McBride, Michael Brown, Tamir Rice and the countless others who have come before them and their families, I thank you for reigniting the passion to finish this book even when the fatigue of working under the heavy weight of this issue would become al-most unbearable. In working with families who have endured such loss, I find that their tragedies place my petty burdens in perspective.

To Michael Smith and to my cousin Brendon Spears (whom I dearly loved and whose loss had a devastating impact on me) and to their families, I can only hope this work provides and/or adds too some perspective although perspective never removes the pain.

I am grateful to Drs. Valata Jenkins-Monroe, Patricia Canson, Craig Adams and Les Campbell (RIP) for nurturing the seed work of this book. I am forever grateful for their foresight, insight and mentorship. Without them, this work would never have seen the light of day and despite my rabble-rousing tendencies they managed to help me get through a very challenging doctoral program.

Back in the day, when I was completing the research that would form the basis for this text (and finishing the last week with walking pneumonia), four young soldiers in the struggle were with me physically and in spirit. Paul Jr., Pcyeta, Pasha and Aziza tolerated my stress level, constant motion and absence and loved me anyway. I thank them for their unconditional love and support. They continue to amaze me! By my side (albeit pneumonia-free) back then, was my wife-to-be, Hilary, who has been a source of support and love through good and frustrating times. This project has endured through the birth of our daughter Kylie, whose entrance was a highlight in the lives of our entire family. Hilary would constantly read drafts and has never complained when I would return to this project even when doing so meant time and space away from her and Kylie and I am grateful for their continued patience through the entire process and being part of this mission.

My big brother, Zeke Jackson, understands this work historically, intuitively and experientially. He is a writer and gifted story-teller in his own right and I am forever appreciative of his love, support and banter (just so it's in print…I finished first!). I am grateful for the love of a host of family members including my brothers Dwayne and Steven, my brilliant nieces and nephews, close cousins Ben Johnson, Derrick Creecy, Hester, Ederine and Alton Alexander and all my uncles, aunts and cousins who shared my path for so many years from Los Angeles to LaPlace and Reserve, Louisiana. I especially would like to acknowledge my Uncle Leland Creecy who provided a structure for my early understanding of manhood and who would provide lessons lasting a lifetime. My Uncle CJ Jackson was our connection to our father's side of the family, including their attitude of "respect not being an option" and I'm thankful for him being there. My Uncle Myron Creecy was the youngest of the crew yet continues to be a rock for the entire family and community and I appreciate him for that.

I would also like to thank my friend and colleague Dr. Raymond Jones who has been a steadfast ear through the years. I have appreciated the variety of support he has offered over the years as well as our ongoing dialogue across a variety of issues. I extend a special thank you to my editor Amy King and her assistant Francinia Williams at Lexington Books for their guidance and solid energy throughout this process. They helped me make tough decisions and I'm sure without their assistance I would not have gained the valuable insights that have made me a better writer.

I cannot close without an acknowledgment of deep appreciation for my mother, Dotty Jackson. Her determined spirit and tenacity is part of my make-up and without her being, who she is, I could not be who I am. She has come through many battles; head bloodied but unbowed. I am blessed to have her still with me and I am forever appreciative of the invaluable gifts I have received from her including her passion for social justice. Raising four sons in south central Los Angeles could not have been easy by any stretch of the imagination and I am forever grateful for her undeserved love and kindness.

Introduction

Black Male Violence, America and Apple Pie

This work found its origins in earlier research designed to test for the effectiveness of exposure to culturally relevant, socio-historically based material on, (1) level of frustration tolerance, (2) the mediation of anger, and (3) level of depression in incarcerated young Black males with histories of violent behavior. The desire to conduct the research came out of life experience and the need to see an end to the tragic cycle of violence we, as African-descended people in America, find ourselves engaged in. An intervention was designed to offer participants a social and historical context for their existence, in America, as individuals of African ancestry and in short, it worked. Exposure to historical viewpoints and to information challenging popular racist notions can have benefits that go well beyond what can be quantified. Reflecting on the importance of having this knowledge of context, two major incidents in my life come to mind that profoundly influenced the development of the above-mentioned study and subsequently, this book. Much later, there would be three separate incidents that would bring me back to the table in a fervent need to complete this work.

The first of two incidents was the murder of one of my best friends. Michael was only eighteen years old when he was murdered. "Big Mike," or "Smith" as we called him, was a captain of his gymnastics team at Washington high school. He had the physique of a body builder and was one of the best gymnasts in the Los Angeles area, already being approached by major colleges. His sisters and younger brothers adored him and we all respected him as we had witnessed his development through the years. Mike's mother made sure he was involved in the church yet he was constantly hassled by the Los Angeles Police Dept. or L.A. Sheriff's. The police in our area didn't bother taking the time to find out who you were or what you were about if you were Black and male. To be physically big and Black was double jeopardy. I was sixteen yet I can remember the day as if it were yesterday. My older brother and I were at the rear of our house playing basketball on the driveway court where probably half of our dreaming, planning and discussions took place. Mike and Ronnie had walked up to ask if we wanted to go with the fellas to Ronnie's cousin's house. The invitation was not abnormal. We were "homies." We had grown up together and would normally accompany each other everywhere we went when possible. This was just as much to look out for each other as it was enjoying each other's company. Gary and Pruitt would be going also. Carl and David couldn't make the trip. As fate (or fortune) would have it, my brother and I had to turn the invitation down due to my basketball game later that evening, as he had agreed to go with me. That night, at the game, my brother and I heard the sound of ambulance and police sirens ringing in the air. We had no idea they were responding to the scene where our friend would breathe his last breath. It all boiled down to a case of mistaken identity. Later, it was explained to me that a car rounded the corner as one of its occupants yelled out a name. As my friends ran for their lives, Mike was caught by two bullets. He died. There was no attempt on the part of police officers to perform CPR or to save his life. His family heard about the shooting and quickly arrived on the scene only to be told that the body that lay underneath the sheet was not Mike but another friend of ours. There was no counseling offered to my friends and me as we grieved the loss of Michael. Instead, we suffered harassment at the hands of the Los Angeles police and sheriff's deputies. At sixteen, I contemplated how ironic it was to be caught between the police, who hated us, and other young Black men who had been conditioned to devalue their own lives and the lives of those who looked like them, us!

The second incident was my being expelled from a new high school unfairly by a racist administrator. I attended a small but popular Catholic high school in south central Los Angeles. Being one of two juniors on the varsity basketball team, my expectations were to have a phenomenal senior year. Athletics were a big part of my life and my potential for participation at the college level was high. As fate would have it, in the last semester of my junior year my school began serious discussions about closing its doors. Most students as well as their parents were not aware of how it would be done but hoped for a merger with another school. The school closed abruptly and for many of us three years of athletic participation went down the drain. We were forced to attend other schools. My new school was also a Catholic school and a former rival. Somehow the administration allowed the student athletes to create a new school rule directed at the new student athletes from my old high school. We were forbidden to wear our letterman's jackets. For me, it was the principle of the thing (isn't it always.) and, of course I had to wear mine. It was so beautiful and at the same time, imposing with the big MC letters superimposed on the left chest area bedecked with gold emblems that told of all the sports in which one had participated. Stars and emblems and scripts and patches all down the sleeves and on the back served notice about this little Black boy from south central. I knew, beyond a shadow of doubt, that my jacket and its proud, indignant wearer were, in fact, "the shit"! I was later attacked by some of the rival students and defended myself. When the principal arrived at the scene of the fight between several opposing students, and me he approached me immediately and yelled emphatically that I was expelled! I was forced off campus and the police were called. The expulsion was later overturned, but the mistreatment left scars. Both incidents aroused anger within me as well as a desire to retaliate.

However, as I contemplated retaliation, three major factors influenced my decision not to do it, possibly setting me on a different course in life from so many others faced with the same dilemma. These three factors were (1) having a natural affection for African-descended people, which was nurtured by my mother and other members of my family; (2) having the ability to weigh the greater potential for harm to innocent people and to my family against the gratification revenge would bring; and (3) having some vague awareness of other systems (educational, legal, criminal justice, economic…) and how they played into the scenario I found myself in, and not wanting to be a victim in what I perceived as a vicious game.

I attribute these three important factors to having a sense of history and to having hope for something better in life. My work with Black youth has convinced me that knowledge of history and being aware of the larger context in which behavior occurs could have an impact on the thinking and feelings that accompany violent behavior. What one knows about one's situation does make a difference. As the ancient Kemetians (Egyptians) would admonish, to "Know Thy Self" is to understand the forces of nature and the universe that is you. And to that end and to those who have given their lives so that we may understand, this book is dedicated.

Many have died to street violence since Mike fell in the summer of 1976. Since then, I have attended too many funerals of those who died too young and heard about too many more I couldn't attend. On October 11, 2004, another bright light was taken away from humanity. Marcel Angelo Johnson was a student of mine. While participating in my Black Psychology class (which was offered once a year), he showed the kind of natural curiosity and true enjoyment of learning a professor wants to see in his students, but sadly enough rarely does. Marcel would sit in class and, like other students, listen and observe in an attempt to feel the professor out. Where is he coming from? Is he for real? Can we trust him? Marcel didn't say much at first, but when he did speak up you could tell he had done some serious thinking about what he was about to bring to the discussion. His writing assignments reflected an even deeper, empathic thought process. I can remember arriving on campus Tuesday morning and being greeted by a student whose sullen and downcast expression told me something of note, something terrible had happened. She explained to me that Marcel had been shot. Hoping against hope, I asked where and what had happened. I was told he was shot near South San Francisco. The perpetrators had jumped out of a van and were wearing some sort of ski masks. The initial shot knocked him down as he and his friend(s) attempted to escape the inevitable attack. The gunmen then ran up to him and shot him in the head, killing him. To date no one has been arrested or charged for this brutal, vicious attack. Everything seemed to be a blur from that point. The pain of promise lost was tempered only by the need to console Marcel's classmates and friends. Fortunately a good friend and colleague, the Reverend Timothy Dupre, worked on campus and was able and willing to assist me in this very daunting task. Tim was and is a friend of Marcel's family and I am forever grateful for his support on and beyond that day as he would later be involved in the wake ceremony, in counseling the family and finally in the funeral event. It was not until the funeral that I realized the impact this young man had had on the community. The church was absolutely overflowing with people. There was no room inside as people lined the stairwells, the line extending to outside the church. I was to speak at Marcel's funeral and had I not informed the usher of this, I in all likelihood would not have been able to enter the main room. I began to learn that this bright young man had reached out and touched many people in the community, young and old. He volunteered as a mentor and tutor. He attended church on a regular basis, served as an usher and sang in the choir. A picture of this young man as a compassionate, cheerful, sincere and considerate human being with a knack for music and writing began to unfold. Quite the opposite of the major media's initial perception, while they anticipated a drug deal gone bad they found none. Where they anticipated gang involvement, they found none. In my discussions with the detectives on the case it is clear that they too have found no connection to drugs or gang involvement. Yes, Marcel's murder now serves as an impetus to complete this work. It is indeed an effort to make sure that (as I gave my word to his family) his death will not be in vain. It is an attempt to actually understand this epidemic of violence in American society. There are too many Marcels out there. Too many families who, on top of the very tragic experience of losing a young and promising son, grandson, daughter, granddaughter, nephew, niece or cousin, must also deal with a myopic, ill-informed, structurally racist media who continue to spill conjecture and prejudiced opinion about real flesh and blood victims; people whom they, as family members have loved and lost to violence. In the name of "good copy" the public is psychologically primed to accept such a tragic loss to the community as Marcel's death, as "par for the course."

The second incident occurred during a local court appearance in the same period of time. As ideas around the impact of Marcel's death and the seeming inability to catch the perpetrators were swirling around my head, I couldn't believe that I was actually being taken to small claims court. I found myself in a courthouse (not my favorite place to be) with a *former* editor (emphasis on the word former because she is an absolute "nutcase" [emphasis mine]) who was trying to get the court to force me to pay for work she had not yet done. Without going into detail, there were a number of options she could've chosen in an effort to work out our disagreement. However she chose to litigate and to go where she was most comfortable. American "justice" systems rarely represent justice to most African-American people. Never having been taken to court, served etc., I didn't know much of what to expect. The nutcase knew all too well what to expect; she was used to it. We both went in and told (or read in her case) our stories and while telling mine I remember mentioning to the judge (who was Caucasian) that the work the editor was to do for me was on a dissertation manuscript. He asked me what the manuscript was about. At that moment I honestly had to stop and think. Not that I didn't know the content of my work but I struggled with how to explain the text in a manner that would not lose the case outright for me! How could I explain to him, in such a vulnerable situation, what the "nutjob" editor well knew, as she had been privy to some of the content; That the work was an honest look at the source of violent outcome including thoughts on how to stem the tide as well as ideas about the way in which America nurtures the very violence it condemns. That it was about the ongoing and pervasive socio-emotional and physical assaults black people endure on a daily basis at the hands of people who look like you and/or who have inculcated your historical cultural mindset to the point where there is no difference, save skin color. That any honest answer to your question in this "hall of hypocrisy" you refer to as justice would act as my own self-condemnation. That the legal/court system you've built your career on, I find to be one of the most historically vehemently violent systems on the planet with all its pretense of mechanized perfection and interest in truth (the trial of the murderer George Zimmerman should be evidence of this for any fair-minded human being). Peace is predicated on justice and justice is predicated on truth. The *truth* is that the American jurisprudence system is no more interested in truth than I am in vacationing in Siberia.

Which brings me to my third incident. Not long ago, I like many others was summoned for jury duty. I live in Oakland, California, and Alameda County so I was ordered to appear at the Alameda County courthouse (I don't know what it was about that academic year and courthouses, but twice was too many!). I had hoped to call in and find I was not needed. When that didn't work out, I had hoped to report in and be dismissed. When that didn't work out, I found myself going back to the main jury cattle call room to fill out a questionnaire the size of a dissertation. The questions seemed so mundane and ridiculous, and the exercise truly tried my patience. "What TV shows do you watch?" "Have you or anyone in your family or friends ever had contact with a police officer?" It was only after sitting in jury selection that I gained a new respect for the mundane nature of the questionnaire.

The defendant was a young (twenty-ish) African-American man who was facing a felony assault charge. The prosecutor was young (thirty-ish) Caucasian (perhaps Italian-American) woman who seemed both very focused and aggressive. The public defender was truly not worth discussing. It was clear, from the outset of this trial, that his role would be quite minimal. The judge who officiated over the process was an African-descended woman and by default, the deck was already stacked.

I was as surprised as anyone could be that I actually made it to the jury box. As the prosecutor went around to briefly interview the potential jurors returning, after each questioning session, to her assigned table to caucus with her teammate, I couldn't help but think that my time here would be short after all. "What city do you live in?"… "What do you do for a living?"…."Do you feel you could make a decision based on the evidence?"…"Would you say you've had positive or negative experiences with police?"…All valid questions, yet questions that would expose me as a peer in the truest sense. And since I knew the prosecution had absolutely no intention of allowing for a true jury of this young defendants peers, I also knew that he had about as much a chance at a fair trial as I had of making it onto this jury. I am a Black man, from Oakland, not financially wealthy, with more than a layman's understanding of this system of jurisprudence; I have experienced it from the inside out, having watched *my* peers suffer at the hands of it. I think *that* would qualify me as this young defendant's peer. Yet as I watched the prosecution prune away potential jurors from Oakland (which is where the defendant was from and where the alleged crime was committed) as well as jurors who looked liked the defendant, it became apparent that the majority of those who remained on the jury would live in outlying areas, would not have a clue of what the defendant's life was like, having nothing faintly resembling a sense of shared experience, would not look like or have a shared ethnicity with the defendant and would have a skewed framework from which to view police activity within the "black" community in Oakland. And all this was before the prosecution even asked about my work experience! In other words, I didn't have a "snowball's chance in hell" of making it on that jury. I was excused and "thanked" for my time (without so much as a fuss from the public defender). Upon leaving the courtroom I felt relieved, knowing that I would not have to go through the motions and summarily get more behind than I already was on work, having my classes cancelled or having to find a substitute. I also felt disturbed because I knew that of the numbers of potential jurors interviewed, I would have made a competent and fair juror. The very process was robbing this young man of a jury of HIS peers right before my (and his) eyes. In that moment, I felt disappointment for him and there was nothing either of us could do about it. It reminded me of an article I had just read regarding the history of unethical jury selection procedures in Louisiana, Texas and Alabama. I know nothing of the circumstances that landed the young man in this situation (as a defendant in a courtroom) but I have no reason to doubt that the outcome was not a good one for him.

Like so many young men, he was caught up, obviously without the knowledge of how to avoid engaging with a system that serves or profits, in one way or another, everyone involved in the system but him. He was part of someone's family as was the alleged victim in this case. Many families are impacted by violence. Often times family members not involved in the violent act end up suffering the most. My family (primary and extended) is no different, having experienced various levels of violence resulting in divorce, imprisonment, and death. To that end, this work is written for those truly interested in facing the reality of violence in our communities and in this society. It is written for those willing to confront the history of violence in the United States and its relationship to violent outcome today. It offers a rationale for understanding the violence we experience...especially where young black men are concerned and it offers a framework for understanding the underlying issues relative to violence as well as some practical solutions.

The ideas put forth go well beyond my vision as I draw from the works of some of the brightest minds in the areas of psychology, sociology, history and neuroscience. Some of these great social scientists, historians and researchers tend to be excluded from the typical academic discourse in the United States, not due, however, to lack of academic rigor. The historians/ researchers I refer to in this text reflect the highest of academic integrity and demonstrate the meticulousness that many of the well-funded think tanks in the United States fall well short of. The "problem" with these researchers is that their work fails to feed the agenda of American hegemony and will not acquiesce to the United States' need to inculcate its own self-indulgent mythology at the expense of young black lives. However, their research and perhaps the ideas reflected in these pages could easily lay the groundwork for much-needed change in this country. With this in mind I hope this book advances the work.

Chapter One

The Problem of Black Violence: The Pain Behind the Statistics

Violence is not new to America. It has been spiraling and growing since this country's inception. At present, violence occurs in America in seemingly epidemic proportions.

Nowhere in the United States is the impact of violent crime and disparity in imprisonment rates more evident than in the population of young Black males. Young Black males bear the brunt of the tragic and destructive outcome of violence and violent crime (Fitzpatrick & Boldizar, 1993; Tucker C., 2003).

Statistics on violent crime as they relate to the Black community, reveal that the problem is even more profound. Not only is the victimization of Black communities a serious mental and physical health problem, but the incarceration rates for Black males have devastating economic and social impact on an already vulnerable Black community. Statistics show that Black households are more vulnerable to crime than are White households (Fingerhut, Ingram, & Feldman, 1992). This may be due to a greater number of Black households than White households existing in high-risk environments. Those environments include social maladies such as greater availability of alcohol and illicit drugs, greater incidents of depression and frustration due to substandard living and rampant unemployment, lack of appropriate police response and protection, and entrenched attitudes and beliefs that support drug abuse and violent behavior. An analysis of the controversial "Stop and Frisk" program provides a window into the negative and deletirious impact institutionalized oppressive tactics can have on a community of people. The Center For Constitutional Rights (CCR) in their report, "Stop And Frisk: The Human Impact" (2012) challenge the constitutionality of this egregious practice and in doing so, brings to light some its damaging effects.

Stops and frisks have a profound impact on the individuals who are subjected to them. CCR heard testimonies from people who had experienced a range of inappropriate and abusive behaviors by police, including being forcibly stripped to their underclothes in public, inappropriate touching, physical violence and threats, extortion of sex, sexual harassment and other humiliating and degrading treatment. These experiences affect people in a multiplicity of ways. While nine out of ten stops do not result in any arrest or summons, everyone subject to a stop and frisk must cope with the emotional, psychological, social, and economic impact on their lives.

It is the emotional and psychological damage that gets very little attention; as if these citizens are not supposed to have feelings about their ill treatment. The alternative is to numb oneself to the traumatic experiences (a topic we shall deal with later), which of course has devastating psychological and emotional consequences. The report further states:

> Stops based on illegal profiling can lead to disproportionate rates of arrests and convictions which, in turn, carry a wide range of damaging collateral consequences (p.5)…Stops and frisks also have an impact that extends to family members of people who are stopped and/or arrested. One woman explained that she often steps in to challenge the police who regularly harass the men in her family because, *"with the men, when they try to speak up for themselves, it makes it worse. The police go hard on them, and find something, some reason, to arrest them."* Children, parents, siblings, and other family members are subjected to seeing their family or community members being routinely profiled, disrespected, assaulted, forced to remove clothing, and/or groped in public by police officers. Some families must live with the added repercussions of the arrest of a family member, a burden that can be particularly heavy for dependent children. (2012, pg. 9)

These community members are expected to endure what no human could tolerate without a significant loss of self-esteem and disruption in normal familial relationships. No wonder so many turn to drugs and/or to some other form of numbing in the face of confronting the true pain associated with such victimization. Many lives have been lost, relationships irreparably damaged, marriages and families torn apart, due to the introduction of drugs and relationships based on drug use. Such was the case of Tina and Joe.[1]

Tina and Joe were high school sweethearts. She was from a church-going family. So was he. Joe had lived with his grandmother for much of his life, as his parents were deceased. Joe attended one of the most notorius high schools in Los Angeles at the time, but managed to stay away from trouble with a focus on basketball and his studies. I met Joe through my older brother as they played on the same basketball team, enjoyed music and excellent sound systems, and ended up being good and close friends. When Joe and Tina got together, they were inseperable. It was obvious to everyone that they loved each other very much.

As their relationship progressed they were soon expecting a child. Joe sought out and got a solid job and bought a car....with an excellent sound system. He was always particular about the listening experience and used to dream of being a DJ live on the radio.

Joe eventually got his own place to live, and he and Tina married and they moved in together. You could tell "little" Joe was pleased. He was a happy toddler and it was nice seeing them as a family.

Tina was always an independent thinker. She had gone through a lot in her life including early sexual abuse and seemed to have come to grips with her early challenges. Throughout their time together Tina maintained her own group of friends. One of those friends introduced her to crack on a social level.

Pretty soon she was smoking crack on a regular basis and those around her noticed clearly that her demeanor had changed. Quite uncharacteristically, Tina was angry and irritable much of the time. A turning point in Joe and Tina's relationship was when Tina smoked the rent money. This led to an argument and Tina threatened to leave, which led to a fight over her leaving. She did leave and after several days of searching for her Joe found her in an alley with homeless others.

Joe tried to separate her from her crack use and her suppliers but she fought it and soon they went their separate ways; their marriage eventually winding up in divorce. Joe would continue to work and maintain the apartment but his emotional pain was evident. He had just gone through experiencing his wife being absent for days at a time while being used for sex to feed her crack habit. Joe's response was unfortunately one that is seen time and again... one that continues the cycle of pain in struggling communities.

Joe began using the drug himself and offering crack for sex with the neighborhood women and their guests. When questioned about his actions, his attitude was one of, "if you can't beat-em, join-em." As a result he, in his anger and hurt, decided to contribute to the bevy of women in south central Los Angeles who had fallen victim to crack addiction and were strung out. Gorgeous women, who the average brother would have to "spit serious game" to, to be engaged long enough to "maybe" get the all important "real digits" (phone number), could be bought for the price of a rock. Seeing otherwise beautiful girls dazed in crack houses, in homes or apartments that weren't considered crack houses or in alleys throughout Los Angeles, trading their bodies was, unfortunately, routine. The prevelance of crack addiction was and still is high and it was and is real.

Joe eventually lost his apartment, became addicted himself and lived on the streets for a while. The last time I saw Joe, he was just out of rehab and trying to turn his life and his luck around. I never saw Tina nor "lil" Joe again. I can only wish them well.

Mr. Melvin was quite a different case. He represented, for me, how wide a reach crack cocaine could have. He was not your prototypical young adult experimenting or enhancing with drug use.

Mr. Melvin lived down the street from my mother in south central Los Angeles. He owned his home, which was connected to a food stand at the corner of the street. In another time period it probably served snacks, ice cream and the like to neighborhood youth. I worked in the community then and I can remember stopping to have quality political discussions with Mr. Melvin every now and then. He was clear and sharp. He was proud of his children and their accomplishments. He always seemed to be a proud man. Within a span of the three and one-half years, upon my return from Chicago, I found him emaciated and near destitute. I was shocked at his condition and embarrased for him once I heard that crack-cocaine was probably involved. Soon after, Mr. Melvin was gone…his house removed from him and abandoned. Crack had become very popular in the early eighties in impoverished communities in south central Los Angeles, Miami and New York. Only later would Pulitzer prize-winning investigative journalist Gary Webb break the story in the San Jose Mercury News regarding the CIA's role in flooding major U.S. cities with crack-cocaine. Los Angeles was one of those cities. The increased popularity of the drug trade among inner city youth only adds an additional layer of complexity to the issues that confront young black men and women.

The complex interrelationship between low self-esteem, psychological disorder, and behavioral dysfunction has been extensively documented in social science literature and is crucial to the analysis of the psychological and behavioral problems of young Black males.

Black males, as they progress through adolescence into adulthood, appear to be more vulnerable than Black females to environmental factors that give rise to such psychological and emotional disturbance. Vulnerability to problems in their families, in their schools, and in their communities is evidenced by disproportionate rates of behavioral and learning disorders, a high incidence of emotional disturbance in delinquents, and high rates of psychiatric treatment among young Black males (Gibbs, 1988). Studies in self-esteem suggest that young Black females generally report higher levels of self-esteem than do young Black males, with an increase in effect with age throughout young adulthood (Rosenberg & Simmons, 1971). This is not to minimize the concern over the reality of growing incarceration rates and abuse among Black women. Women comprise the fastest growing prison population in the United States. From 1997 to 2007, the number of women incarcerated grew by some 832 percent (Misplaced Priorities; 2011) and many of those women were likely to have experienced past physical and sexual abuse. Still, for young Black men, there are no extant social institutions they can turn to for redress. Jewell Gibbs (1988) states:

> Since studies suggest that Black male children as compared to females are given less nurturance by their parents, treated more harshly by their teachers, discriminated against more by employers, and treated less favorably by nearly every other institution in American society, it is reasonable to infer that their lower level of self-esteem is the inevitable outcome of their persistent, differential and demeaning treatment (p. 237).

In his book *Fatherless America* (1995), David Blankenhorn considers the case of Joseph Chaney Jr., who garnered national attention, making the front page of the Wall Steet Journal. The young Chaney was thirteen years old at the time and, by edict of the grand jury, was to be tried as an adult for armed robbery. Blankenhorn goes on to explain that Chaney had been arrested sixteen times since the age of six, was being raised (along with two other brothers; each with a different father) by his mother, who has struggled with drug addiction, and that the family had received support services from a number of programs (pgs. 26-27).

Blankenhorn is making the argument that perhaps of all the contributing factors to youth violence, cited by various research studies, the one factor most of these studies overlook is the absence of the father in the home. To his credit, Mr. Blankenhorn does recognize the very complex nature of the problem and that young Joseph Chaney did face numerous issues in his life. He makes a compelling argument for the importance of fathers in our children's lives. Even though Blankenhorn offers a thorough treatment of various perspectives on an ideology of the meaning of fatherhood (in its various forms) in American society, replete with meaningful studies, there is one area of discourse that seems to be missing from the discussion; especially when it comes to the Black youth he cites in a number of his tragic examples. The matter of "context" appears to be suprisingly vacant from the discussion. More specifically, the issue of historical context when it comes to the dynamic of current day Black fathers and their children has no place in Mr. Blankenhorn's work at all.

There are certainly opportunities to deal with the important issue of historical context throughout the text. Perhaps there are inherent conflicts of interest when one is attempting to base a set of assertions on a value system that in reality juxtaposes itself to criticize or castigate that which it creates.

The Carnegie Corporation study summarized recent research finding frustration, lack of social skills, poverty, drug and alcohol abuse, physical abuse and neglect, violent television programming and video games and absence of effective mentoring programs to name a few. Blankenhorn states that the APA's commission on Violence and Youth in their 1993 report on Youth and Violence made similar findings including factors like access to guns, involvement in gangs, social and economic inequality, and prejudice and discrimination among others.

The brilliant philanthropist, activist and author Randall Robinson certainly provides a solid example of not shying away from the necessity of dealing with historical context in our attempt to gain an understanding of such very difficult issues. In his work, *The Debt* (2001), Mr. Robinson illustrates the life of a young man whose "dead end crisis" could represent the plight of millions in America.

In so doing, he retraces the representative history of this young man's great-great-grandfather, including being born and dying a slave, laboring for the benefit of many including his white owner, the ship builders, ropemakers, sailors and countless other businesses that serviced and benefited from the cotton trade built on the backs of slaves. He includes the impact of the Civil War and the defacto "freedom" of the slaves...the movement from Slave Codes to the Black Codes; from the evils of the oppressive segragated south to struggles to move towards the Voting Rights Act of 1965. Mr. Robinson in summary, writes:

> They had been declared free—four million of them. Some had simply walked off plantations during the war in search of Union forces. Others had become brazenly outspoken to their masters toward the war's conclusion. Some had remained loyal to their masters to the end. Abandoned, penniless and unskilled, to the mercies of a humiliated and hostile South, millions of men, women, and children trudged into the false freedom of the Jim Crow South with virtually nothing in the way of recompense, preparation, or even national apology...It is from this condition that today's black male emerged....The black male is far more likely than his white counterpart to be in prison, to be murdered, to have no job, to fail in school, to become seriously ill (Robinson, pp. 209-217)

Randall Robinson got it right; "parallel lines never touch, no matter how far in time and space they extend." Mr. Blankenhorn's approach, although chock full of important statistics can not and will not produce results for the Black father. It may, at best, highlight the need for "traditional" fathering, but what is traditional for the Black man in America? For the Black male, context is everything.

In addition to health and economic concerns, the impact of violent crime as it relates to the number of Black males in the prison system, has had tremendous impact on the social fabric of the Black community. The over representation of Black males in the prison system renders a staggering number of Black males unavailable as fathers and family/community leaders. Prison involvement often leaves such men unavailable for credible employment, advanced education, professional licensure, and community defense against discriminatory policy and practices. One may consider the question;

how many Black teens are even aware of the importance of voting or professional licensure? All too often, by the time they are aware, significant numbers of Black youth are already young adults with criminal records. By then it is too late. It appears some in congress intend to keep it that way. Young Joseph Chaney's case occurred in Florida. One need only look at the events in Florida around the year 2000 presidential election to grasp the gravity of this situation. The numbers of Black men and women legally excluded from the voting process were staggering and for many, so was the outcome.

An extensive 1990s study on the status of African-American males in California noted that while comprising only 3.7% of the state population, African-American males constituted 33.8% of the prison population and only 1.7 and 2.1 % of the enrollments at the University of California and California State University systems respectively. Males comprise better than 90% of the total prison population. And this cannot be explained simply by population growth. When we examine the history on prison population growth in the United States we see that between the years 1926 and 1986 the recorded number of Black prisoners grew at a much faster rate than the recorded number of White prisoners. The recorded number of Black prisoners in 1986 was almost nine times larger than the number recorded in 1926, whereas the recorded number of White prisoners was three times larger, and the number of other races was five times larger (Langan, 1991). This increase cannot be explained by the change in population of the United States. The Black population grew 2.6 times larger, from 11 million to 29 million, between 1926 and 1986. Within the same time period, the White population grew 2.1 times larger, from 100 million to about 200 million and other races grew 21 times larger, from less than 1 million to 17 million. Also within the same time period, the imprisonment rate for Blacks rose, while the imprisonment rate for Asians, Native Alaskans, American Indians, and Pacific Islanders dropped.

Not much has changed and if anything the situation has only worsened with time, as funding priorities relative to the construction and maintenance of prisons, for many states tend to steadily increase. In 1992, the U.S. spent $94 billion on the justice system, with $32 billion going to corrections, a 356 percent increase over what was spent in 1980, some $6.9 billion. A recent CNN (2012) broadcast reported that the state of California now spends 1,370 times more on prisons today than in 1980, that the state of New York has seen a 127% increase in prison spending since 1987 and that the U.S prison population has grown 700% since 1970. Legislation also appears to continue to support the imbalance of Blacks tied up in the prison system. According to a recent NAACP report (Misplaced Priorities; 2011), in 2009 as the United States experienced its deepest recession in thirty years, funding for education declined while thirty-three states spent more of their discretionary dollars on prisons than they had the year before. In the last two decades, state spending on prisons grew at six times the rate of state spending on higher education. And when we take a good look at who is filling these prisons, the disparities in enforcement of drug laws becomes glaring. Although members of all ethnic groups use illegal drugs, African-descended americans are imprisoned for drug offenses at 13 times the rate of White Americans. From 1985 to 1995, State incarceration of African-Americans on drug charges increased 707 percent according to the Justice Department, while it rose 306 percent for Whites. As a matter of fact, 58% of the U.S. prison population is African—descended and Latino, while they comprise only one-third of the nation's population. In addition, legislation around drug use and proliferation of illegal drugs says a great deal about how we as a nation respond to these social and mental health issues. It is truly a shame that almost a quarter of all those in the prison system (more than 500,000 people) are there as a result of a drug conviction. What's more, the huge increases in the prison population have not been responsible for the lion's share of crime reduction, calling into question, the value of prisons as a deterrent (Pew; 2009).

It is clear that the criminal justice and prison systems perpetuate unequal treatment of Black males. Prisons in the United States are a final receiving point for many Black males who have endured a lifetime of differential treatment. And once there, they are more likely to experience lethal violence and further victimization in that system. We cannot lose track, however, of their importance to this vast system, and to its maintenance and growth. Every industry needs a product and the prison industry is no different.

Emerge Magazine in their landmark exposé "Crime Pays. Cashing in on Black Prisoners, Caged Cargo" (1997) blew the lid off what has become one of the largest, fastest growing industries in America, the prison industry. In this article, Davidson writes, "the fear of crime feeds a self-perpetuating cycle for the prison-industrial complex. Politicians create harsher penalties as communities compete for facilities and big financiers underwrite prison construction bonds" (p. 36). He goes on to cite the participation of companies like Goldman Sachs, Prudential Insurance Co. of America, Smith Barney Shearson Inc., Merrill Lynch, Westinghouse Electric Corporation, Alliant Techsystems Inc. and Minnesota Mining and Manufacturing Co. as a few who represent wall street's interest in the sordid business of prisons. Companies like Corrections Corporations of America, Wackenhut Corrections Corporation and U.S. Corrections Corporation are but a few of the privately held prison companies in the U.S. who find crime a very profitable business.

According to Davidson, "feeding that correctional-industrial complex is a series of laws, policies and practices in the criminal justice system that make young Black people, in particular, fodder for the selling network. Criminal behavior, combined with a system biased against the poor and Black, provides the industry with a steady stream of human cargo" (p. 36).

Commenting on a damaging videotape that surfaced of Missouri prisoners being mistreated and brutalized in a Texas facility in Brazoria County, Missouri state Representative Charles Troupe stated "This is the Rodney King tape of corrections…But most of America thinks prisoners are no longer human…But the thing that frightens me most is that when you start having prisons for profit and Wall Street is intricately involved in prisons, then the politicians are going to change all of the criminal codes in the country to fill every prison that Wall Street builds" (p. 43). The 'Three-strikes' sentencing bill has been a case-in-point. Before it was adopted it was heavily pushed and promoted by the CCPOA (California Correctional Peace Officers Association), which gave funding to more than sixty legislatures who would vote on the three-strikes bill.

A Bureau of Justice Statistics report (Langan & Graziadei, 1992) in its conclusion that violent offenders are more likely to be Black, raises several key issues such as why, when Black people account for only 12% of the total population in the United States, do Blacks account for approximately 46% of the prison population and upwards of 50% of those inmates sentenced for violent crime. In addition they represent 74% of those sentenced to prison for drug possession while being only 13% of all monthly drug users? Black males accounted for 90% of the Black prison population, and 54% of those males are below age of 29 (Nobles, 1989). This disparity indicates a pervasive bias in the justice system. The disparity between White youth and Black youth referred to court for drug violations is also discouraging. For example, between 1985 and 1986 court referrals for drug violations for White youth dropped by 6%. By direct contrast court referrals for Black youth increased by 42%. Certainly, one could speculate on the role of differential sentencing laws for crack versus powdered cocaine, in producing these desparities. Yet with such large disparities, the American system of jurisprudence itself, must be called into question. Recently, investigators have broached the topic. Abrams, Bertrand and Mullainathan (2012), in their study entitled "Do Judges Vary in Their Treatment of Race?" cite that in 2008, 38% of sentenced inmates in the U.S. were African-American and that African-American males were incarcerated at six and a half times the rate of White males. The authors go on to ask the question of whether or not these differences in incarceration rates "merely reflect racial differences in criminal behavior or are they also partly an outcome of differential prosecution or sentencing practices?"

Questions remain. Questions like why Black adults are four times as likely as whites and nearly 2.5 times as likely as Latinos to be under correctional control? What is the social impact on the Black community, and what are the health implications for the Black community? Who are the victims? How do these statistics influence strategies for violence prevention? Strategies like the development of mentoring and rites of passage programs.

Mentoring and rites of passage programs (which imbue young men and women with cultural philosophy, values, and principles to develop youth in ways consistent with cultural models of manhood and womanhood) are examples of strategic interventions that impact the negative behavioral effects of differential treatment. Most African-American manhood training models focus on facilitating awareness of African culture and values and teaching African-American history. Their intent is to enhance the participant's self-concept and to promote healthy and positive behavior in young African-American males, and they are largely successful. Little is known, however, of the cognitive or affective mechanisms by which African-American males who participate in such courses, are influenced in a positive direction. Questions remain as to what extent the positive changes are attributable to transferential issues between instructors and participants, individual styles of presenters, the actual information being presented, or format of the material. A key issue in the utilization of such programs in the field of psychology is the question of their clinical relevance.

NOTE

1. Tina and Joe are pseudonyms.

Chapter Two

Historical Context of Violence among African-American Youth Racism and its Expression Within the U.S.

"If you do not understand White Supremacy (Racism)...what it is, and how it works—everything else that you understand, will only confuse you."
—Neely Fuller, Jr., The United Compensatory Code/System/Concept

It is difficult to understand the causes of violence or comprehend the potential for its treatment without placing such violence in its historical context within the United States. Black youth live and survive in a society which has subscribed to particular views, attitudes, ideas, and assumptions about people of color, in general, and Black people in particular. When the attitudes and assumptions emanate from a racist psycho-structure, the outcome of interactions between individuals and between individuals and institutions can be abusive, debilitating, and destructive. Racism has enjoyed a myriad of expressions in America. It assumes both overt and covert (often insidious) forms and is largely responsible for the self-hatred, dehumanization, anger, and frustration associated with Black-on-Black violence.

America, however, has been mostly in denial of its racist origins, racist history and of the modern-day racial dynamic that is interconnected with its racist past. The defensive mechanism of denial is understandable. No collective group of people desire to claim and accept that their ancestors were responsible for the rape, torture, bestiality towards and murder of native people of color in the Americas, in the continent of Africa and elswhere. To think that one's ancestors found amusement in the humiliation, denigration and sadistic torture of the very people who once greeted them with warmth and openness, for a person of conscience, would be debilitating. It is no wonder American historiography must be completely revisionist. Native Americans therefore, must be represented as savages...initiating the practice of scalping (when there is no record that Native Americans in North or South America were ever infatuated with caucasian hair. The founding fathers must be represented as men of conscience...truly invested in the concept of freedom, justice and equality while many of them owned human beings and were realistically not vested in these concepts outside of their own self-interest. The Trail of Tears...the tacit support for the racist South African regime against the legitimate aspirations of the South African people to be free...the use of dogs, tear gas, bombs and guns against ordinary people marching to exercise their legitimate right to vote...the list of contradictions go on and on. Many social scientists, including author/researcher Dr. Joy DeGruy-Leary have looked at Leon Festinger's theory of cognitive dissonance to explain the cognitive mechanisms at work which allow the white american collective community to live with cognitive tension created by such opposing beliefs and actions. Dr. Leary says:

> The greater the difference between our actions and what we think about ourselves, the greater the cognitive dissonance and so, our discomfort....During the past 500 years Europeans have spent significant resources to 'prove' Africans and those of African descent are inferior. The difference between the actions of the Europeans (i.e., enslaving, raping and killing) and theeir beliefs about themselves (i.e., 'We are good Christians') was so great and the cognitive dissonance so painful, that they were obliged to go to great lengths in order to survive their own horrific behavior. Chattel slavery and genocide of the Native American population were so un-Christian the only way they could make their actions acceptable, and so resolve the dissonance, was to relegate their victims to the level of sub-human...With respect to the genocide of Native Americans, and the enslavement and later oppression of those of African descent, the history we in this land learn has been greatly sanitized. (54-73)

Clearly, the Christian tradition of whites had to be quite different and opposed to that of the Christian tradition of African-descended people or First Nation peoples here in America as they adopted what was taught to them by white christians. Clearly the slave would be praying to a different God than the slave master. Even the Black church today, with its emphasis on non-violence and collective love (to include thine enemies) can be seen as arguably diametrically opposed to the historic ethos of the American Christian tradition.

In line with this analysis I am inclined to think of extant Christianity as it relates to the White American collective community as being structured along and supported by four pillars. These pillars are what drive, motivate and insure the survival of the White American collective community. These four pillars form the bedrock for the propagation of White Christianity all around the world and despite the deep-seeded belief in the importance of "righteousness" as a virtue these four pillars drive the historical behavior of White Christianity. They have been and remain: 1) the Primacy of Wealth; 2) the Devotion to Capitalism; the Propogation of the Mindset of White Supremacy and 4) the Supremacy of Armament.

A more detailed discussion could be had along each of these pillars however for the sake of the scope of this work it is suffice to note that these pillars have driven the historic behavior of White Christianity towards people of color around the world and Africans in particular. Here, in America we need look no farther than the contradiction within its operationalized constitution.

The American psychological adjustment necessary to justify such divergence between its stated purpose (its constitution) and its behavior would have to be extreme. The respective roles of political, artistic and scientific intstitutions in shaping the psychology of adjustment within the White American collective community would have to be huge. And indeed they have played a pivotal role in crafting the justification of such abhorrent behavior. This certainly includes relabeling the victims to accommodate justifying sadistic behavior (JBHE, 2006, DeGruy, 2012).

The White American collective community literally jumped at the opportunity to claim an American "post-racial" society upon the election of Barack Obama as the 44th President of the United States. Although 'openly' Black, President Obama was in fact, not the first president of African-descent (ref), nor did he prove to be the harbinger of a post-racial America. His presidency was met with one of the most obstructionist congresses in the history of the congress. Many rationalizations for opposing the Black (actually bi-racial) president were made by congressmen/women, senators and red-state governors, who were particularly careful to stay away from the president's "race" as a factor. However as these individual leaders began to ramp up their opposition to proposed legislation, even they themsleves had produced because those ideas were embraced by *this* president, it became apparent that race was a real and tangible factor in their almost fever-pitched opposition to him.

Of course, the White American collective community is in complete denial. Attempts at the national level to have a dialogue on race have been stymied... even after the eloquent and extremely generous speech the president gave on the topic in 2008. However, if we move away from the relative safety of placing racism somewhere on the laundry list of items in need of improvement/fixing (along with a living wage and marriage inequality etc...) as we move towards a more egalitarian society and strive to understand what "it" really is, such anger, obstruction and vitriol begins to make more sense. We begin to understand that "it" brought the nation within a hair's breadth of placing an arguably sociopathic candidate (Jackson, 2012) at its helm.

From a psychodynamic perspective, racism can be understood as a low level defensive or adjustment mechanism that is used by a collective group of people much in the same way defense mechanisms are utilized by individuals to deal with very real anxiety (Comer, 1969). Dr. Francis Cress-Welsing adds depth to this explanation, providing detailed perspective on how the defense mechanisms of repression, reaction formation, projection and displacement underlie the development of an uncontrollable sense of hostility and aggression on the part of whites...an attitude that has "continued to manifest iself throughout the history of mass confrontations between whites and people of color" (Cress-Welsing, 1991).

Dr. Cress-Welsing's *Cress Theory of Color Confrontation* is in part, based on the work of the great social-scientist Neely Fuller Jr. who offered, in his work *The United Independent Compensatory Code/System/Concept; a Textbook/Workbook for Thought, Speech and/or Action for Victims of Racism* (white supremacy), an early structural explanation of racism as a global system of organized behavior for the purposes of white supremacy domination in all areas of human activity. As such, she offered a functional definition of racism as...

"The local and global power system structured and maintained by persons who classify themselves as white, whether consciously or subconsciously determined; this system consists of patterns of perception, logic, symbol formation, thought, speech, action and emotional response, as conducted simultaneously in all areas of people activity (economics, education, entertainment, labor, law, politics, religion, sex and war). The ultimate purpose of the system is to prevent white genetic annihilation on Earth—a planet in which the overwhelming majority of people are classified as the non-white (black, brown, red and yellow) by white-skinned people. All of the non-white people are genetically dominant (in terms of skin coloration) compared to the genetically recessive white-skinned people." (ii).

Whether conscious or unconscious in its motivation, the assault and battery of the young teenager, Darren Manning, by Philadelphia police is but another example of racially driven violence. It is the type of violence that clearly stems from hatred and quite possibly a fear of genetic anihilation. Darren Manning, on January 7, 2014, was on his way with some teammates to play in a high school basketball game. They were wearing their team uniforms, hats and scarves. Darren is a sixteen year old model student at the Mathematics, Civic and Sciences Charter School. The boys were approached by police and started to run, however Darren started to run and stopped because, as he reported, he "had done nothing wrong." What followed was an unnecessary beating and groping session at the hands of the Philadelphia police. He was cuffed by the officers, groped and grabbed by his testicles by a female officer who squeezed and pulled so hard she ruptured one of his testicles, requiring that he go to the hospital where surgery was performed the next day. Doctors warned his mother of the distinct possibility that he may never have children. Of course, the officers charged this straight "A" student who, according to the school's prinicpal, had never had a disciplinary problem in his high school career, with resisting arrest. Witnesses at the scene have corraborated the young man's story while Darren's mother, Ikea Coney, blamed herself for teaching him to respect the police and not to fear them reasoning that perhaps if he had run his life would've been different. She was quoted as saying "I'm just grateful they didn't kill him."

Dr. Cress-Welsing is not the first mental health professional to express the belief that white people could benefit from having such an awareness of the motivation behind behaviors that even they don't quite understand or that mass therapy is in order and should be on the table. One did not have to be a social-scientist to understand that all the bloodshed, pain and struggle of the civil rights activities, the horrific and visible assassinations of that era, the Watts riots or the L.A. rebellion did not amount to a change in the White American collective psyche in matters of race (or white skin privilege).

There has never been a national movement or process created to help White America come to terms with and treat what many see as the illness of racism. Racism is understood by many clinicians (and especially Afro-centric psychologists) to be a psychiatric disorder (although not currently included in the DSM V) in that it fits the diagnostic criteria for mental disorder. According to the late Dr. Asa Hilliard (1978, 1991), racism emerges as an adaptive process which stems from operating a system of domination, he called the *Dynamics of Domination* a series of processes utilized by europeans to subjugate entire populations of non-white people. These processes were 1) the erasure of African memory, 2) the suppression of the practice of African Culture, 3) to teach white supremacy, 4) to conrol the institutions of socialization, 5) the control of wealth and 6) physical segregation. With these historical activities, Europeans engaged in order to conquer the continent and to enslave people. According to Dr. Hilliard (1991), "if one operates a system of domination based on these activities, one must eventually confront the truth. The only way to be consistent in applying the rules of such a system is to bend the truth. Over time it results in an adaptive process we call 'racism' which is really a mental illness." Manifestations of racist behavior as a result of domination are based on the following criteria for mental illness:

1. Denial of Reality
2. Perceptual Distortion
3. Delusions of Grandeur
4. Phobias in the face of difference
5. Projecting Blame

Recent research (Goff et al, 2014) published by the APA found that Black boys as young as ten may not be viewed in the same way as their white peers relative to childhood innocence. In a four-part study including police officers and non-police officers, researchers found a disturbing picture of the effects of racism on Black children in the U.S. The study provides evidence that Black children are afforded the benefit of innocence to a lesser extent than children of other races. Black boys are misperceived as older and seen as more censurable for their actions relative to peers of other races and evidence points to these racial disparities being tied to implicit dehumanization of Black people. This tendency to dehumanize Blacks was not only predicitive of racially disparate perceptions of Black boys but predicted racially dispar-ity in police violence toward Black children in the real world. Finally, re-garding what the research suggests, the authors state "if, as Alice Walker says, 'The most important question in the world is, "Why is the child cry-ing"?' then for Black children, the most important answer may be that they cry because they are not allowed to be children at all" (pp. 15-16).

Clearly, if left untreated these psychological processes can lead to disor-ders with serious behavioral consequences. All communities suffer in the process. These consequences include, but are not limited to, violent outcome and the reactionary violence we see manifested in the behavior of some Black youth.

WESTERN IMAGES OF BLACK MALES

From a clinical standpoint, an understanding of history helps answer the question of why Black youth practice violence. To appropriately consider violence among Black males in America we shall look at the establishment of America in relationship to Black people.

America is a country born of violent conquest. Countless authors have documented the legacy of brutality and murder left by Europeans in their conquest of what was, to them, the "New World." This trail of blood stretches from Africa through South America to North America and beyond (Diop, 1992; Wilson, 1990; Zinn, 1985). Acquisition of land by European invaders meant the subjugation of the people on that land. Along with this expansion came European dogma, myth, and philosophy to justify such ac-tion. In support of this rapid expansion, the practice of slavery needed to be institutionalized and sanctioned by church and state (Stampp, 1956).

Much has been written on the institution of slavery. For our purposes, it is sufficient to say that for Africans, slavery was an extremely violent and dehumanizing institution. In order to justify slavery, those who were to be-come victims of the most brutal chattel slavery in history needed to be reclassified and dehumanized by the European. African studies scholar Wade Nobles (1989) discusses this process:

> The negative images and societal projections on the self-image and self-esteem of Black men began with the historical contact between Africa and the West. It is within this contact that one finds the philosophical basis for racist behavior. During this contact the one outstanding sign having special meaning was the intended meaning of the "Negro." It is extremely important to recognize that the concept and meaning of "the Negro" is an entirely different and distinct ideological and philosophical construct from the image and meaning of "the African." Literally, from the beginning of human consciousness to the advent of "the Negro" the position of the Black man and woman and the relationship between the African and the non-African was the opposite of what it is now. The meaning of the African in the historical consciousness of the European, for instance, was (up until the advent of the "Negro") associated with high culture, superior civilization and sophisticated human systems of organization (i.e., governance, commerce, family, religion etc. (p. 5).

Historically, Caucasian (European) people viewed African (Black) people with awe and respect (James, 1985). European world domination, with its insatiable and impenitent economic imperative, however, required the destruction of African civilization and history, and redefinition of "the African." This required the exchange of admiration and respect of "the African" for the image of the disrespected and worthless "Negro."

There is no question the orientation of Europeans towards Africa and Africans went through a drastic turn. In elementary school, I can remember learning about the period of the "Dark Ages." It was taught to us as a blip on the historical map with no sense of how Europe went into relative darkness nor how Europe came out of such dark times. We were never taught that the Moors went into an illiterate and backwards European nation, bringing structure, science, art and education (Van Sertima, 1992). By doing so they would give Europe the tools it needed to rise out of the muck and mire of their own debased existence. This part of history was purposely omitted from our education. It remains omitted from most television representations of that period. Very few of my students have ever heard of the Moors; fewer still have ever been made aware of their contributions to the world. It is not surprising given the Eurocentric nature of our educational system and Europe's revisionist historiography.

Racist philosophical doctrines of human domination and exploitation were produced by Europeans against the backdrop of a permanently installed Judeo-Christian/Greco-Roman philosophical ideological base, and Europe emerged from the dark ages with a new interpretation of history steeped in Eurocentrism. This era signaled the creation of the philosophical foundation of racism for the purposes of economic exploitation. The ancient African belief that man could exist either in a state of ignorance or in a state of enlightenment with the purpose of life being to grow from ignorance to enlightenment, was conveniently translated by European philosophers into metaphors of "Darkness" and "the Light." Subsequently, ignorance came to represent Darkness and enlightenment to represent Light. Darkness and Light were then exchanged for characterizations of "Evil" and "Goodness." Evil and Goodness were eventually symbolically represented as "Black" and "White." Ancient Europeans, in turn, placed the people of the world into categories of color, with Caucasian (White) people being the good (superior) and people of color (non-White) being the bad (inferior) (James, 1985; Nobles, 1989; Williams, 1976; Wilson, 1993).

It is important to note that the *images of Black males* created by American society and western culture have been and continue to be extremely negative and destructive. Reclassification of the African as the Negro, with its evil, inferior and salacious connotation, directs the perceptions and choices of all people relative to the value and images of Black men and women. These negative images are responsible for a host of popular and accepted notions and ideas about Black males which have tremendous economic, social, and political impact on Black men around the globe.

For example, negative ideas, or fixed false beliefs about Black males (i.e., to be a Black male is to be a person who is ignorant, lazy, shiftless, irresponsible to his children, unsupportive of his mate, who wants something for nothing, who never tells the truth, who has athletic superiority but intellectual inferiority, who is sexually aggressive, materialistic, deviant, and violent), are ideas reflected everywhere in this society. These negative images proliferate from television to elected government officials who support and structure law. They have a history of legal support as reflected in laws like the "Jim Crow" laws which made segregation the written and enforced law of the South. Many of those laws were only recently abolished, while some are still quite functional. As Michelle Alexander has so eloquently presented in her work *The New Jim Crow*, the names have changed but the game is still the same. "What has changed since the collapse of Jim Crow has less to do with the basic structure of our society than with the language we use to justify it" (p. 2). This system of apartheid is alive and well and functioning as a powerful means of exploitation and financial growth for American corporations, whether or not they experience direct participation in the exploding prison industry (as mentioned in chapter 1).

These images have not only impacted Caucasians in this country, but have had tremendous impact on people of color. For Black youth, and Black males in particular, the effect of a host of negative variables (negative images, fixed false beliefs, negative perceptions, poverty, frustration) interacting in the context of a hostile and racist environment, has been a type of mental slavery, and a self-fulfilling prophecy (Akbar, 1980; Mills, Dunham, & Alpert, 1988; Nobles, 1989).

Even more devastating has been the instillation of the mindset of devaluing Black life, and the evolution of the mentality of self-hatred. Western media as a structural system, unfortunately, has had a long and devastating history of propogating imagery responsible for such debilitating programming. More on this topic will be covered in the chapter that follows, but suffice to say, the *machine* represented by the Western entertainment complex with its long tradition of expropriating culturally defined artforms (especially those artforms arising from the inner-city streets, ghettos and poverty stricken plantation communities of Black folk) for the express purpose of economic exploitation and social engineering, has left no stone unturned.

It can be argued that, in only one generation, the artform, Hip-Hop/Rap (which some of us helped create and shape), has been co-opted to further propogate this irrational and devastating mindset. This is not to say, Hip Hop has not struggled to make a comeback. The struggle continues as mainstream/conscious artists like Nas, Talib Kweli, Lupe Fiasco and non-mainstream/conscious Greydon Square among others endeavor to break through the industry mire to stimulate thought and motivate dialogue around critical issues. They harken back to the days of mainstream/conscious Grandmaster Flash, Public Enemy, KRS-1, Chubb Rock, X-Clan and non-mainstream/ conscious westcoast artist, Paris, who articulated with clarity the pain and suffering of a generation, offered historical context and suggested revolutionary thinking and action. This was before the comedization of Hip Hop and its avid misogynistic striving, so aptly covered in Byron Hurt's 2006 award winning documentary, *Hip Hop: Beyond Beats and Rhymes*.

Clearly, Hip-Hop/Rap as an artform holds tremendous potential to do great good within various communities and especially with Black youth. It has been a positive force for intervention (as evidenced by this author's surgical use of Hip-Hop/Rap in crafting intervention later described in this text). However, if it is to reach its true potential for transformation, as an artform, we must unleash its potential from the fetters of an industry whose historic framework has been inimical to the people from which the artform was created. Certainly, Shakespeare and the Europeans of his time had no problem accepting the prestige and position of the character, Othello. This reshaping of the image of Black/African/Moorish men was something new in the long stretch of recorded history.

These, rather new-world, formative and destructive frameworks for interpreting reality have never been fully addressed by those who created and benefited from the institution of slavery and were certainly never addressed through the emancipation of the slaves.

As we turn our discussion back to the resulting mindset of devaluation, adjunct is the fact that the poverty and powerlessness of Black youth exist in an atmosphere of hopelessness, alienation, and frustration reflected by growing antisocial behavior. Such antisocial behaviors are often blamed on Black youth who are written off as being culturally deprived, intellectually deficient, and pathologically deviant (Gibbs, 1988). The current violence among African Americans represents a new dimension of oppression which serves a similar function as slavery. In American society, African-American violence serves the function of justifying and rationalizing White supremacy. This is born out of the fact that African Americans have become the most visible destroyers of their own people.

American imagery of African Americans has been quite successful in creating the perception that African Americans are unable to look over their own affairs and require outside intervention. Those who set policy for crime reduction/prevention and those who develop remedies for the consequences of violent behavior are no less susceptible to the negative images and perceptions discussed above. Many of the remedies, as a result, are short-term Band-Aid type solutions that are quite temporary, very perishable, and/or ineffective in addressing the underlying causes of frustration, depression, and anger in Black males. Thus, violence prevention/reduction strategies will continue to fail if efforts are not undertaken to address the adverse effect of cultural racism (Oliver, 1989).

BLACK MALE VIOLENCE: CAUSES AND OUTCOMES

As a legacy of slavery, Black-on-Black violence is a common response to the frustration, internalized anger, and depression felt by African-Americans. Hutchinson (1990) notes that no matter how much Blacks were victimized by White violence, Blacks were not permitted to retaliate. In slavery, Black males who wanted to protect themselves and their families and/or who attempted to escape to freedom, were frequently severely maimed or murdered. Men and women who resisted or questioned authority were treated severely, as examples to the Black community. This model remains in place today, as severe treatment, brutality and murder of Black citizens (and especially Black youth) by Caucasian citizens including those authorized to "enforce the law" remains an ever present reality.

James Allen's expose, *Without Sanctuary; Postcards from the Edge*, brought awareness of the horrors of lynching and the horrific mindset of the many Caucasians who participated in such gruesome acts, to many who had never been exposed to it. Allen's (a self-described collector) expose/exhibit was controversial as it drew critcism from both ends of the spectrum; from those who percieved the exhibit to be insensitive to the black community to those who felt the history should not be dredged up and that it should be put behind us. However, many expressed appreciation at Allen's willingness to allow the world to see his collection of postcards and at once come face to face with the reality of an America that would find amusement in the horrific nature in which so many people were murdered. The idea that white Americans would create and send postcards of human beings lynched, beaten and burned alive defies American sensibility and American mythology. But old habits die hard.

Rodney King, in 1991, knew that a DUI would most likely land him back in jail but he had no idea that deciding to end the chase would lead to him being almost beat to death by several LAPD officers. He also had no idea that his beating was being videotaped; nor did the perpetrators of this crime, the cops. These bullies in uniform, also had no idea of the fury their crime and subsequent acquittal would help unleash. The L.A. rebellion (riots) often misunderstood as the Rodney King riots were set off at a flashpoint on Florence Ave near my childhood home. Abusive police officers were on the scene and doing what they are known for in the Los Angeles area. The people had had enough and those officers and their reinforcements were over-run. This happened to coincide with the notorious Simi Valley verdict which acquitted all officers involved in this horrific beating. Tensions were already high, fueled by the murder of 15 year old Latasha Harlings about one month earlier, by Korean liquor store owner, Soon Ja Du. Latasha was shot in the head by Soon Ja Du over a dispute over a bottle of orange juice. The murderer was sentenced only to probation. This was an appalling message to the Black community about the value the judicial system and by extension, the Korean and other Asian communities placed on the life of a Black child.

The King verdict was a slap in the face to the Black community in Los Angeles and to people of conscience all over the country. Most L.A. residents are well aware of the history of mistreatment at the hands of the LAPD. For us, the Rodney King beating was nothing new; the difference was that the act was finally caught on tape. The judicial system worked for these white officers, as it has so many times before this incident and in a way that it is doubtful to ever work for members of the Black community. The trial was moved out of the community where the crime was committed and into a community where the officers involved would have the benefit of a jury of *their* peers. In other words, people steeped in denial about racism, who would do anything to protect the mythology that drives their belief regarding who these men (who they commune, worship and recreate with) are and in the inherent debasement of those who are victimized by them.

Given the inherent and historic bias in the judicial system relative to the treatment of police officers and those who are victimized by them, the Simi Valley verdict was innevitable. So was the level of frustration, anger and depression within the Black community at large and in Los Angeles. Having no outlets for retaliation, the community imploded and the LAPD became scarce as they could not handle the response and would more than likely become targets. Unfortunately, a lone white truck driver, Reginald Denny, stuck in the mayhem, would be among the many, attacked and injured. It should be noted that at least half those arrested and full one-third of those killed during the days of rioting were Latino/Hispanic. Also the individual who rescued Mr. Denny was an unarmed Black man from the neighborhood, Bobby Green Jr. who saw the attack on television. In the end the violence and destruction threatened to move outside of L.A. proper, Korean store owners took up arms, national guard troops were called in to gain control, over fifty people were reported dead and over 2,000 injured and the police chief, Darryl Gates, a long time member of the LAPD brass and resident racist, resigned.

These types of violent acts are meant to serve as an example to others in the Black community who would think about defying the ultimate authority of a person with a badge. The badge as experienced in many Black communities means power over life and death let alone authority over one's body and person. As a father of two Black young men, I have always been keen to the tightrope they must walk, especially during the teen years and their period of young adulthood. It is indeed the very same tightrope I walked in my youth. They are both kind young men…strapping and handsome, intelligent and possessed of the qualities of leadership. They also happen to be principled individuals as many young Black men are. Being principled sometimes means these self-respecting young men must decide whether or not to defend their already fragile self-respect in a scenario with police that could easily cost them their lives where unnecessary use of force is all too often at issue. The tightrope they must walk between violence at the hands of those youth who fall into thuggery and the violence they will more than likely experience at the hands of those who are sworn to protect and serve them (the police) is a tenuous one.

The violent interactions in my youth, between me and my friends and members of the L.A. Vikings gang within the L.A. sheriff's department are fresh in my mind, as are the countless incidents of demeaning and negative treatment at the hands of LAPD officers. We were always under threat of being shot to death by these *"enforcers of the law"* and at times we would petition them to remove the gun belts and batons and meet us in the alley…an offer they never took us up on!

I have long advocated to police departments that their officers cannot "serve and protect" people they do not love and whose culture they do not respect. No better illustration of this statement can be found than the example of the case of Oscar Grant.

The film *Fruitvale Station* gave the world a look at the interactions and events in a day in the life of the young Oscar Grant. In the film we are treated to a perspective the public rarely sees in the media…a victim of police violence as a regular human being. We follow Oscar as we watch him engage with his family, including his 4 year old daughter, with co-workers and friends. We watch him as he struggles with decisions about how to support his family in a way that allows him to steer clear of jail. It is New Year's Eve and we watch as he contemplates his mother's suggestion (for he and his friends) to ride the BART (Bay Area Rapid Transit) train to see the fireworks display in San Francisco. She doesn't want him on the roads. They can be *dangerous*.

The Shooting of Oscar Grant

The facts of the shooting were taken not only from witness testimony, but a BART platform surveillance video and cell phone videos taken by five BART passengers. All of the videos were admitted into evidence.

In the early hours of New Year's Day 2009, Oscar Grant boarded a BART train in San Francisco with his fiancée, Sophina Mesa, and several other friends. The group was bound for the Fruitvale BART station. The train was standing-room-only crowded with New Year's Eve celebrants.

As the train approached the Fruitvale BART station in Oakland, an argument broke out between Oscar and a fellow passenger. A tussling match ensued and spread into a large fistfight, involving at least ten men. Passengers used the train intercom to report the fight to the operator, who in turn contacted BART central control who apparently contacted BART police, with a report of "a fight at the Fruitvale BART station in the train's—lead car, no weapons, all black clothing, large group of B[lack] M[ales]" (I must stop here to note that as a psychologist, the idea that any department, charged with the duty of 'public safety,' would use terminology commonly utilized to denote a bowel movement [BM] as a descriptor for Black males is alarming and abhorrent).

The train reached the Fruitvale station and stopped at the platform. The doors opened and the fight stopped. BART Police officers Anthony Pirone and Marysol Domenici were on the street level of the station. According to the police report, Pirone went up to the platform and saw five African-American men, including Oscar and Michael Greer, and one woman standing on the platform by the lead car and talking. As Pirone approached, Oscar and Greer got back on the train. According to a bystander, Pirone appeared to be agitated and said, "This train isn't fucking going anywhere, I'm not stupid, I see you guys." Pirone then ordered the three men who remained on the platform to stand against the platform wall and keep their hands visible. He pulled his taser and pointed it at the men as he ordered them to the wall. Pirone called Domenici and told her to come up to the platform, where he instructed her to watch the detained men against the wall.

Pirone ordered Oscar off the train. By one account he said, "Get off the fucking train, otherwise I'm going to pull you out." By another account he said, "Get off the train motherfuckers." By his own account, Pirone said, "Get the fuck off the train." Grant got off the train. Pirone took Grant over to the three detainees and shoved him against the wall. The men sat down after being ordered to do so by Domenici.

Pirone went back to the train for Greer and ordered him out, saying "Get the fuck off my train." Pirone denied using profanity when he ordered Greer off the train, because of the presence of female passengers. Greer did not comply. Pirone said, "I've asked you politely. I'm going to have to remove you in front of all these people now." Pirone then grabbed Greer by his hair and the scruff of his neck and forced him off the train. Train passengers described Pirone as hostile, angry, mean, and aggressive. One passenger said Pirone acted "like a punk." Several passengers testified that in their opinion Pirone used excessive or unnecessary force, or that his behavior was excessive. Oscar and the two other young men jumped to their feet and shouted, "This is fucked up, this is fucked up," to which Domenici responded, "stay out of it." Pirone approached one of the young men and told him to "shut the fuck up." A cell phone video and other testimony shows Pirone striking Oscar with his fist shoved him against the wall and forcing Oscar to his knees. A passenger's video shows Pirone drawing his taser and pointing it at the young men. Oscar pleaded with Pirone not to tase him saying "I have a daughter!" Domenici drew her taser and pointed it at the others, who kept their hands up and pleaded, "don't tase me." According to a BART surveillance video, Johannes Mehserle and his partner, Officer Woffinden, arrived on the platform at 2:08:27 a.m. Mehserle drew his taser and pointed it at the detainees, including Oscar. The red laser sight was trained on Grant's chest and groin. Woffinden drew his baton and ordered people away from the area. At 2:09:24, Officer Guerra joined the defendant to help guard the young men. Oscar answered a call from his fiancée, who was on the street level, and said, "They're beating us up for no reason. I'm going to call you back." Sophina thought he sounded scared.

Referring to Oscar, Pirone said, "that motherfucker is going to jail for—148" (a reference to Penal Code section 148, resisting a police officer). Pirone testified he gave the order to arrest Oscar and Greer. When he heard he was going to be arrested, Grant stood up and asked, "Who can we talk to?" A cell phone video shows Pirone grabbing Grant and forcing him back down while grabbing his head.

At this point, three officers—Mehserle, Pirone and Guerra—were dealing with the five detainees and two officers—Domenici and Woffinden—were keeping the crowd of bystanders away from the area.

Grant was kneeling on the ground while Pirone was yelling in Oscar's face, "Bitch-ass nigger, right. Bitch-ass nigger, right. Yeah." Mehserle stepped behind Oscar and grabbed his hands as Oscar fell forward onto the ground. Pirone used his knees to pin Oscar's neck to the ground. Oscar pleaded, "I can't breathe. Just get off of me. I can't breathe. I quit. I surrender. I quit." According to defendant and murderer, Mehserle, he ordered Oscar to give up his arms, presumably so he could handcuff him and repeatedly pulled at Grant's right arm, which apparently was under his body. At 2:10:49, two more BART officers, Knudtson and Flores, arrived on the platform and ran to the area. Knudtson tackled one of the bystanders after he (or the person next to him) threw a cell phone at Domenici and Woffinden, who were still keeping the crowd at bay. Flores took up position next to Domenici and Woffinden to help them keep the crowd, who were apparently appalled at the heavy-handed treatment of the young men, back. The crowd although vocal, was nonetheless peaceful. Woffinden testified he never drew his firearm because the crowd's behavior did not warrant such a response.

Meanwhile, the police report states Mehserle was heard to saying, "fuck this. I can't get his hands, his hands are in his waistband, I'm going to tase him, . . . get back." A cell phone video shows Mehserle tugging three separate times on his handgun, unsuccessfully trying to remove it from his holster. On the fourth try, he was able to remove his handgun. He stood up, held the weapon apparently with both hands, and fired a bullet into Grant's back. The time was 2:11:04. Video evidence clearly shows that Oscar's hands were cuffed and behind his back as he lay prone (face-down), and defenseless, while he was shot in the back.

Shortly after the shooting, Mehserle talked to Pirone on the platform and said, "I thought he was going for a gun." In the minutes after the shooting he had several conversations on the platform with Pirone and three other officers, and said nothing about mistaking his handgun for his taser. Later, at the station, he cried and told a support person, Officer Foreman, that he thought Grant was going for a gun. He did not say he mistook his handgun for his taser. Yet the "mistaken taser" explanation would be the cornerstone for his defense.

Oscar Grant was taken to Highland Hospital. He had a single gunshot wound that penetrated his right lung causing excessive blood loss. He would be pronounced dead approximately four hours after having surgery.

As the videotape of Oscar's murder went viral, what followed was an eruption in the city of Oakland in a momentous expression of outrage and frustration at the system's maneuvers to protect the murderer Johannes Mehserle who fled to Nevada where he was arrested. Like so many white police officers, who *work* in the inner cities and reside well outside the environments they work in, Mehserle was from the Napa Valley area. As communities organized in protest, Mehserle's supporters were overwhelmingly white and were based in overwhelmingly white Walnut Creek. However, they were eclipsed by, overwhelmingly, diverse crowds of supporters for justice for Oscar Grant.

What followed was a process that rivaled any other major miscarriage of justice on U.S. soil. Like the defense for the perpetrators in the Rodney King case, Mehserle's attorney petitioned for and received a change of venue citing the inability to receive a fair trial for his client in the city where the crime was committed. The trial was moved to Los Angeles where no African-Americans were chosen for the jury. The trial judge (Robert Perry) introduced a gag order on the proceedings, not allowing cameras or media in and then by all accounts from Oscar Grant's family, proceeded to preside over a courtroom infused with bias and racism.

Mehserle, who had been in protective custody for almost a year and who was on trial for murder, was convicted of a much lesser included charge of involuntary manslaughter. To make matters worse, the defense went on to file a motion in request of a new trial, which, to Oakland residents and Oscar's supporters, amounted to another slap in the face. Mehserle's defense presented him as an honorable peace officer while concealing the fact that only two months before killing Oscar Grant, he was involved in beating, kicking and using excessive force against another Black man who merely voiced his displeasure with the lack of assistance he was receiving as a victim of vandalism. All in all, Mehserle served only eleven months in "special" custody before walking out a free man after murdering Oscar Grant in cold blood. A Grant family member was quoted as stating that this sentence "demonstrated just how racist this criminal justice system is."

As poignant an example of racism, on all levels (personal, interpersonal, cultural, an institutional) as the Oscar Grant tragedy represents there can be no clearer expose of the dynamic of white-skin privilege, the demonstration of the delusional quality of white American collective community thinking, the impact of negative imagery of Black young men and of the failings of the criminal "injustice" system than the tragedy of the Trayvon Martin story.

Trayvon Martin

While Floridian Marissa Alexander, an African American mother and victim of domestic violence, faces spending the next 20 years of her life in prison for shooting warning shots into a wall, the murderer George Zimmerman walks freely. Certainly not worse (what could be worse than the taking of an innocent life) but more outlandish, if there is such a thing, was the murder of Trayvon Martin, a 17 year old boy in Sanford, Florida on February 26, 2012. Trayvon Martin was pursued by an armed gunman, George Zimmerman. Trayvon was carrying iced tea and a pack of Skittles candy he had just purchased from a 7-Eleven store. While talking on the phone to his girl-friend, he explained to her, his voice clearly reflecting the anxiety of one being chased, that he thought this guy (Zimmerman) was following him.

Minutes later, Trayvon would be shot dead, murdered by Zimmerman.

Minutes before Trayvon was killed, Zimmerman, who was armed, had called police stating that Trayvon looked "suspicious." Trayvon was unarmed and walking back to his father's home, when he was accosted by Zimmerman.

Despite being instructed by the police dispatcher not to follow Trayvon, Zimmerman proceeded to confront and fatally shoot the boy in the chest within a matter of minutes. Despite Zimmerman admitting to following, confronting, and killing Trayvon, he has was not arrested or charged with any crime.

At the crime scene, Sanford police, in an appalling display of police work, botched their questioning of Zimmerman, refused to take the full statements of witnesses, and pressured neighbors to side with the shooter's claim of self-defense. As it turned out, the Sanford police department had a history of failing to hold perpetrators accountable for violent acts against Black victims. The police misconduct in the Trayvon Martin case was just another example of the Sanford police department's systemic mishandling of such investigations.

The case was compromised from the beginning. When Sanford police arrived on the scene, Zimmerman was first approached by a narcotics detective and not a homicide investigator; he was peppered with questions rather than allowing him to tell his story without prompting; in addition an officer "corrected" a witness giving a statement that she'd heard Trayvon cry for help before he was shot, telling her she had heard Zimmerman instead.

Sanford police department's history includes a pattern of not prosecuting when the victim is Black. In 2010, the white son of a Sanford police lieutenant was let go by police after assaulting a homeless Black man outside a downtown bar. In 2005, two white security guards killed a Black teenager. One of the perpetrators was the son of a Sanford police officer. The pair were arrested and charged, but a judge later cited lack of evidence and dismissed both cases.

Even in the face of witnesses who were certain the shooting was not in self-defense, who stated that the screams for help ended with the gunshot and even though Trayvon was unarmed, the State Attorney's office, after rubber-stamping the Sanford police's despicable investigation, claimed that there was not enough evidence to support even a manslaughter conviction.

It was not until Trayvon's family and hundreds of thousands of people around the country took to the streets demanding justice for Trayvon that the Department of Justice considered looking into the case.

In the process of publicizing the Trayvon Martin case, Florida's notorious "Shoot First" law, which takes a shooter's self-defense claim at face value, was placed front and center in the American discourse. In addition, people around the world became aware of this law, heavily supported by the gun lobby, which incentivizes law enforcement *not* to make arrests in shooting deaths that would lead to murder charges in other states.

What followed can only be described as legal "Kabuki" theatre. Public outrage drove the police department to finally arrest Zimmerman and the district attorney's office to bring charges. Zimmerman's defensive team put on a show for the media and to a jury of six women that, again, included no African-Americans and only one ethnic minority. Later one minority juror would state that she was severely troubled because Zimmerman "got away with murder."

Writer Susan Abulhawa captures the tragedy of this miscarriage of justice and the institutional racism that supports it…

> The 'not guilty' verdict for George Zimmerman's killing of Trayvon Martin did not come as a surprise to African Americans or anyone familiar with the US justice system. Ultimately, the trial was theatre because the decision to clear Zimmerman was effectively made the same day that he shot Trayvon, a 17-year-old African American.

> Footage of the 'arrest' of Zimmerman showed him walking into the police station without the cuts and marks seen later in the photos. The police knew, from Zimmerman's own 911 calls, that he had stalked Trayvon. They knew that Zimmerman assumed that Trayvon lived in the neighborhood (in the interview Zimmerman said he continued to follow Trayvon to 'get an address'). They knew, from one of the witnesses who called, that someone was yelling desperately, heartbreakingly, for help.

> Zimmerman's father would claim those calls were from his son, not Trayvon, even though George Zimmerman himself said during the interview that it didn't sound like his own voice. Further, and I wonder why this question was not asked: Why would someone with a gun scream with such terror for help? (Incidentally, the cries for help stopped abruptly when Trayvon was shot.)

> Other than photographing Zimmerman's face, the police did not collect forensic evidence from him, despite clear inconsistencies in his story during the initial interview on February 26. They didn't dust his hands for gunpowder residues. They didn't scrape his nails or hands for DNA evidence that could have clarified the nature of the physical struggle between him and Trayvon. They didn't collect urine or blood samples to see if he was doped up on drugs. They didn't take his clothes for evidence. They let him go home.

> But the primary reason the police didn't arrest Zimmerman is that in the current power structure, black bodies are worthless and expendable. Not only did the police allow a murderer to walk out of the station with his gun that night, but also they lazily bagged Trayvon's body as 'John Doe' and carried on. Not one officer thought to knock on a few doors in that gated community to try to locate the young man's family, who were surely worried that their son

had not come home. We know all too well that things would have gone very differently had Trayvon been white....The contempt, the disregard, and the disrespect for the black body run through this whole case. It runs through this country and transforms itself to adapt to the times. It moved from slavery to Jim Crow laws and lives now in the so-called 'War on Drugs' that targets, by legal design, African Americans. The evidence of racism in these laws is abundantly clear. (*Trayvon Martin Case a Travesty of Justice*, Al-Jazeera America)

Walking home from the store shouldn't cost you your life, but in a world when Black youth are routinely assumed to be violent criminals, being randomly killed is a constant danger. Only months after Trayvon Martin's shooting another young Black teenager, Jordan Davis became a victim of senseless murder in Florida at the hands of a White man, Michael Dunn. Dunn initially claimed "Stand Your Ground" rights while firing into a car containing three other young Black teens. All were unarmed. He didn't approve of the type of music they were playing in their own car nor of the volume at which they were playing it. Ten of Dunn's bullets from his 9mm pistol hit the vehicle even as it fled, three of them hitting Jordan. He would fatally wound 17 year-old Jordan Davis who died at the hospital. Dunn's defense team did not use the "Stand Your Ground" law but certainly used its premise in front of a mostly white jury that included *NO* Black men.

On a Saturday evening, February 15, 2014, the jury failed to reach a verdict on the murder charge in the Michael Dunn case. While the jury did find Dunn guilty of three charges of attempted murder and one charge of firing into a vehicle, the judge declared a mistrial on the charge of murder in the first-degree; another slap in the face for Black families and a clear indication of the inherent injustice of the "justice" system.

Indeed Dunn felt justified in murdering an unarmed young man who by all accounts was a good kid, as he has taken on the role of victim stating that he is a "survivor." As for the so-called justice system as it relates to homicide across racial lines, Roman, reporting on behalf of the Urban Institute (2013) found that in states with "Stand Your Ground" laws, when the shooters are white and the victims are black, 34% of the resulting homicides are deemed justifiable. When the shooter is black and the victim is white only 3% of the deaths are deemed justifiable. A 2013 study by the institute (Roman, 2013) found substantial evidence of racial disparities in justifiable homicide determinations in general. While controlling for all other case attributes, there is a 281 percent greater chance that a white-on-black homicide is found justifiable than if the homicide is white-on-white and those differences are exacerbated in "Stand Your Ground" states.

As recently as November of 2012, 19 year old Renisha McBride was shot in the face at point blank range by another White male (Theodore Paul Wafer). Renisha had been in a car accident and approached Wafer's porch looking for help. It is unknown what outcome the "justice" system will create for Renisha's family. However, if recent history is any indication, justice may be far away.

As of the writing of this manuscript, the family and supporters of Eric Garner, a 43 year-old Black man, husband and father of six, who was attacked by at least four NYPD officers and murdered on July 17, 2014, are hoping for justice as they await a scheduled grand jury hearing. It appears Mr. Garner had just broken up a fight when he was approached by police officers who claim they approached him because they suspected him of selling individual cigarettes. They entire tragedy, fortunately was captured on film as officer Daniel Pantaleo proceeded to place Mr. Garner in a choke hold and with the assistance of other officers, took him down, choking him to death. All this, while Mr. Garner continued as best he could, to explain that he could not breathe.

The current mayor, Bill DeBlasio was quoted as stating that he was "absolutely committed to ensuring that the proper reforms are enacted to ensure that this won't happen again." Further, he stated "we all have the responsibility to work together to heal the wounds from decades of mistrust and create a culture where the police department and the communities they protect respect each other." This author believes the above statements mistakenly places the Black community on par with an historically abusive police force in sharing responsibility for such abuses. One also wonders just how far down the rabbit hole the mayor and his associates are willing to go to "ensure the proper reforms."

Only a few weeks later an 18 year-old, unarmed, Black young man would be murdered in cold blood by a Ferguson, Missouri police officer. On August 9, 2014, Michael Brown was fatally shot by a white officer later to be identified as Darren Wilson. Wilson did not try to resuscitate Michael Brown, nor did he call for medical help. Young Michael Brown's dead body was left exposed and in the open for hours despite protests from the community members on hand, to cover him up. Community members gathered in peaceful protest, later that evening, at the site of the killing and at the police department. As demonstrations remained largely peaceful they were met by officers in military-grade riot gear and in armored carriers, using tear gas and rubber bullets, exercising excessive force in clear violation of international law. What followed was the use of sound cannons and equipment fit for a war zone as well as the arrest and suppression of journalists as the entire tragic event exploded onto the world scene and was picked up by the international press, America's dirty laundry fully aired as it claims to be a beacon of freedom, justice and equality. Caught up in this mix was St. Louis alderman, Antonio French, who had been meeting with community members and documenting police actions. French was also arrested by police and jailed "because he didn't listen."

Eventually state highway patrol Captain, Ron Johnson, a Black man and Ferguson native would be brought in to take charge of ground operations and the area would experience an immediate decrease in tensions while almost one week after the shooting, the Ferguson police department would finally release Darren Wilson's name. Conveniently and simultaneously they also released surveillance footage of a young man they claimed to be Michael Brown, shoplifting at a convenience store. Although the justice department had expressed its wishes that the Ferguson police department not release the video due to concerns it would re-ignite tensions, they made the decision to do it anyway in what only could be understood as an attempt to sabotage the work of Captain Johnson and his officers and to provide cover for the murderer Darren Wilson. They would admit, later, that Officer Wilson had no knowledge of Michael Brown being a suspect when he shot the victim. The good will that Capt. Johnson created was predictably undone as protests continued, police continued to attack and threaten journalists and protesters alike (some of which was caught on camera) and Gov. Jay Nixon would ultimately impose a curfew and call in the National Guard. Things have calmed down as of this writing but the story of Ferguson and the killing of Michael Brown are far from over.

As the story and filming of yet another police killing in St. Louis of a young Black man, (who by most accounts was suffering from some type of mental illness) Kajieme Powell, emerges, the unfortunate truth of the matter is that police departments across this nation are not only resistant to change, they actively work against positive and productive change. Buttressed by policeman's unions, associations and by politicians, the criminals, abusers, murderers and bullies within these law enforcement agencies remain protected. While police departments are allowed to continue to refuse revamping their screening and evaluation processes to include screening for racist ideation, implicit pejorative attitudes and authoritarian personalities, they also enjoy the protection of politicians who ensure there remains NO accountability (personally or otherwise) for the most grievous violations of human dignity. What's happening in Ferguson is a sham...and the people know it. The police department went into immediate protection mode for the murderer of Michael Brown. Everything they have done...from failing to immediately order his report to hiding his identity to choosing a secret hearing by grand jury to maintaining the racist apparatus that includes the current county prosecutor...has been in the service of protecting the murderer of Michael Brown and ensuring the status quo in Ferguson and in the surrounding areas.

The frustration, anger and rage that grow out of these experiences are multifaceted and palpable. The stress that accompanies the inability to find resolution when such egregious acts are allowed to proliferate can be devastating. The frustration of being constantly misperceived according to the negative imagery projections of the white American collective community (so much so that the very lives of Black youth are at risk) is not unlike the tremendous frustration, anger, and rage which grew out of similar experiences that pepper America's racist past.

These experiences were never allowed expression toward the Caucasian people who were the source of the anger. The outlets for such rage were few. They were found in work, at home, or in the Black community, thereby forcing Blacks to internalize their anger and displace their aggression onto other Blacks. History shows that the penalties for Blacks when violent toward other Blacks were far different from penalties for Blacks when violent towards Caucasians. Crimes committed by Blacks against Whites were met with death or long imprisonment, whereas crimes by Blacks against other Blacks were ignored or lightly punished. This helped to instill in Blacks the belief that violence and repression against other Blacks was socially approved (Hutchinson, 1990; Stampp, 1956). An outcome of these inculcated belief systems can be seen in the high incidence of Black-on-Black crime in the inner-cities. A high incidence of homicide is found in urban areas which characteristically have high population density, high unemployment (especially among Black youth), and poor housing. It follows that such conditions serve to produce the frustration, depression, anger, and lack of self-esteem which may be associated with high incidence of homicide. These conditions account for a big part of the everyday experience of young Black males.

ON CONSIDERING CULTURAL AND ETHNIC FACTORS IN BLACK VIOLENCE

Cultural and ethnic factors must be considered in the discussion on violence, because of their influence on the expression of aggression and anger. Wade Nobles, a leading scholar on African-American history and psychological development, states, "When the symbols, rituals and rites of one's culture lose their legitimacy and power to compel thought and action, then disruption occurs with the cultural orientation and reflects itself as pathology in the psychology of the people belonging to that culture" (Nobles, Goddard, Cavil, & George, 1987). Violence among young Black males can be seen as emanating from a skewed view of themselves solely as descendants of slaves. Many Blacks, young and old, believe that Blacks have not contributed to civilization or achieved greatness in areas other than sports and entertainment, and that Blacks can never amount to much. This negative self-image—the devastating and dehumanizing effect of systemic, institutional, and interpersonal racism in American society—has manifested itself in the development of intense self-hatred and self-destructive behavior patterns in Black youth.

In most instances behavior can not be divorced from attitudes, beliefs, emotions, and cognitions (Kazdin, 1987; Spivak, Hausman, & Prothrow-Stith, 1989). Since behavior is often a consequence of these variables, self-destructive behavior may be seen as a result of negative attitudes, beliefs, and cognitions about oneself. The mediation of anger is an important additional aspect of violent behavior and aggression, and is key to the negative effects of anger suppression.

Homicide is the leading cause of death for Black males age 15-24. These youth are more often murdered by each other for reasons that include street holdups, drug dealing, sexual jealousy, and gang fights. As far back as 1980, Hawkins (1986) reports that 44% of Black victims were killed by Black offenders. It is indeed tragic that Black males have a one in twenty-one chance of being murdered in their lifetime, as compared to a 1 in 104 chance for Black females, a 1 in 131 chance for White males, and a 1 in 369 chance for White females. It is interesting that although Black males comprise only 6% of the total population of the United States they account for over 34% of all murder victims. It is telling, that Black men in Harlem have less of a chance of reaching the age of sixty-five than men in Bangladesh (Lusane, 1991; Nobles, 1989). Black youth are socially, economically, and politically disenfranchised, which leads to an increased victimization rate. In addition, Black youth as a whole are perceived as violent and prone to crime. This generalized perception of all Black youth as antisocial is part of the victim-ization process which serves as a source of frustration for Black youth. Per-vasive racial bias in arrest, prosecution, and imprisonment, and media sensa-tionalism fuel this perception (Lusane, 1991; Nobles, 1989). When White and Black teenagers commit the same crime, the justice system (including the police and courts) is seven times more likely to charge Black teenagers with a felony and to convict and jail them. The rate of incarceration for teens was 44 to 1 for Blacks versus Whites in 1990 (Stark, 1990). Twenty years later, not much has changed. The idea that most illegal drug use and sales happens in economically disadvantaged, people of color communities is a fiction. However, despite this fiction, Black men have been admitted to state prison on drug charges at rate greater than 13% higher than that of White men. When it comes to the racial disparity in drug sentencing as a part of the "War on drugs," we see that one in fourteen Black men was locked up compared to 1 in 106 White men. The statistics are worse for young Black men between the ages of twenty and thirty-five with 1 in 9 being locked up in 2006 and far more being under penal control (Alexander, 2012). Consequent-ly, 25% of all young Black males are either on parole, probation, or incarcer-ated, compared to only 6% of young White males. No wonder Black youth must work through intense frustration. Understanding the context is every-thing.

Chapter Three

Violence Among African-American Male Adolescents and the Role of the Media

In 2011, about 14,610 victims of homicide were reported in the United States making this the lowest number of homicide victims reported since 1968 and marking the fifth consecutive year of decline in known homicides (BJS, 2013).

However, for African-American males, the statistics on violence and assault remain ominous when it comes to homicide. Although statistics show that for the period between 1992–2011, the homicide rate in the United States declined by some 49% (BJS, 2013), for African-American youth, the statistics on homicide victimization still show a level of risk that far exceeds that of the White population and figures for all other ethnic groups. For several decades the figures associated with homicide victimization among Black males relative to Black females, White males, and White females generally agree that the Black male has a lower life expectancy than any other sex and ethnic group (Fitzpatrick & Boldizar, 1993; Hammond & Yung, 1993; Nobles, 1989; Spivak et al., 1989). In the mid 1980s the morbidity rate for Black males was almost twice that of White males and Black females and three times that of White females. Although the period between 2002 and 2011 (where the homicide rate for Blacks was 6.3 times higher than that of Whites) had seen an overall decrease in homicide rates among all races with the most dramatic decrease among American Indian, Alaskan Native, Asian, Native Hawaiian and Pacific Islander (a 33% decrease) populations, the gap in life expectancy between Blacks and others, however, seems to be widening. Two decades ago, national figures showed that a young Black male was six times more likely to be murdered than a young African-American female, nine times more likely than a young White male, and twenty six times more likely than a young White female (Center for Disease Control, 1990; Issacs, 1992). In the last decade, statistics show that homicide rates increased for both white and black males after age fourteen and into the early twenties with some very significant differences. The homicide rate peaked for white males at age twenty (11.4 homicides per 100,000) whereas the homicide rate peaked for black males at age twenty-three (100.3 homicides per 100,000). The murder rate for black males remained upwards of nine times higher than the rate for white males (BJS, 2013). The peak homicide rate for black females was four times higher that the peak rate for white females.

Even more glaring was the 55% rise in homicide rates for African-American young males reported by Center for Disease Control. It is indeed telling that in some areas of the United States the rate of homicide actually exceeds the casualty rate among soldiers in Vietnam (Issacs, 1992; Lusane, 1990).

There are other facts that should not be ignored. Between 2002 and 2011 the homicide rate in largest urban areas decreased by almost one-half. Also when statistics on murder are reported the demographic data on homicide offenders often goes unreported largely due to offender information being "missing" from the FBI's Supplementary Homicide Report (SHR). This data is missing either because the reporting law enforcement agency did not identify a suspect or because they simply did not report known information on the SHR. In 2011 a whopping 31% of homicide victims had missing information on the demographic characteristics of sex, race and age for homicide offenders. In addition, when the victim was black the demographic characteristics of the offender was missing 40% of the time compared to if the victim was white (23%) and 36% of the time when the victim was male as compared to female (16%). It is also interesting that during the first term of Barack Obama's presidency, black males were victims of a higher proportion of homicides involving guns than in the early nineties while the proportion of white male victims for the same period decreased. The same can be said for black females.

Although the rise in incarceration rates have little to do with the rate of violent crime, the young Black male remains truly at risk. I am reminded of a moment where our family was watching the show, *American Idol*, (our daughter and daughter-in-law are fans of the show. I am more or less forced into viewing it!). It was time, in the competition, for the contestants to perform a brief piece for the judges. A young man explained he would perform a piece he had written in honor of his brother who had been killed only weeks before. It was only when the young man began to perform the beautiful piece that my daughter-in-law put the pieces together as she threw her hands to her face in shock. This young man Savion Wright was the brother of Alfred Wright, a Black young man who was a husband, father and physical therapist and who was murdered when his pick-up truck broke down in Hemphill, Texas.

Alfred was experiencing trouble with his truck so after pulling into the parking lot of one of the few local grocers on an isolated stretch of route 87, he phoned his wife to give her directions to the store. His wife phoned his parents who took off to get him and found when they arrived that he was not there. The rest of the story is shrouded in mystery.

The next day, the search for Wright, turned up his wallet, watch, clothing and his keys at a nearby ranch. After the fourth day the Sabine County Sheriff (Thomas Maddox) called off the search saying to the family, "your son's just a missing person. My guys are tired. We've exhausted our resources and funds. We're done," according to the family's lawyer Ryan MacLeod. The sheriff would go on to claim that "likely drug related" and that Wright ripped off his clothes due to hallucinations. The family found this rather strange given the indication that the sheriff's daughter probably knew or knew of Alfred in their respective health care capacities.

The family would go on to conduct their own search and eighteen days after Alfred Wright went missing, they found him in the same area the sheriff's search party claimed they had searched. His lifeless body was found with only his boxer shorts on, with one sock and his tennis shoes on. His phone was tucked in his sock. Several of his teeth were missing, his ear was missing and his tongue was cut out and his throat was slit. There was very little decomposition compared to most bodies left in the elements for eighteen days.

The Sabine County Coroner's office his death "accidental" and in an eerie echo of the sheriff's prediction, claimed based on a toxicology report that his death was due to a combination of cocaine, meth and amphetamines. The family did not buy it. They had never known Alfred to use drugs. He was church-going and there was no personality change to indicate he was on drugs. Being wisely suspicious of the investigation, the family hired an independent pathologist who ultimately found, contrary to the Sabine County medical examiner, what appears to be "severe trauma to the neck and head."

Congresswoman Sheila Jackson Lee announced that the United States Department of Justice will now open an investigation into the death of Alfred Wright. Her petititon outlined eight points where she believed that "overwhelming and credible evidence" was ignored by the Sabine County Sherriff's initial "*investigation*," including questioning the decision to call off the search for Alfred Wright after only three days even though some of his personal effects had been found. Wright's own family found him just yards from the initial search command post. Another point cites the contradicting autopsy reports. The initial autopsy failed to address the straight-line cut to his throat. As of this writing, the independent autopsy has not been finalized due to Sabine County authorities being slow to return photographs from the initial autopsy.

The Congresswoman raised the issue of the documented racial violence towards African Americans in the area of South East Texas. The Wright family is from Jasper, Texas (45 minutes away from Hemphill) where in 1998 a Black man by the name of James Byrd Jr., was walking home when he was approached by three White men (one of whom he was acquainted with) who offered him a ride home. James got into the bed of the pick-up truck and was driven to an isolated, wooded road and beaten severely. He was then chained to the back of the truck by his ankles and dragged for more than four miles before his murderers dumped his torso in front of an African-American cemetery. Police would find his remains in eighty-one places along the road. At least, by the end of the next day, all three suspects were in custody.

All indications in the Wright case are that the sheriff's office is involved in a cover-up as they appeared to be assembling their story while conducting their *search*. No doubt the Alfred Wright case, without intervention from Congresswoman Jackson-Lee and the Department of Justice, would be one of the many cases with missing offender data on the SHR.

THE MEDIA AND VIOLENCE

It must be noted that the use of media has had tremendous impact on the perceptions and acceptance of violence in America as well as the perpetuation of images that reinforce false beliefs about Black males (Spivak et al., 1989). Despite the data and the known history of violence in the United States clearly identifying Black people in general, and Black young men in, particular, as victims of that violence, American media overwhelmingly continues to perpetuate imagery representing Black youth as violent criminals.

The need to acknowledge and address the devastating impact such imagery has had on the American psyche as well as their socio-political implications and consequences can not be overstated. White american collective community members tend to operate from a framework that views Black young men as part of a criminal class. Thus, when violent interaction occurs between Black young men and members of the white community (as in the cases of Trayvon Martin and Oscar Grant), that community, including the media structures that provide information and perspective have a difficult time not adopting an automatic defensive posture relative to the white individual involved in the altercation. This knee-jerk response includes wondering what the young man must've been doing wrong regardless of whether or not the white perpetrator is a cop or a civilian.

This delusional quality exists in the perception of many Americans despite claims of "post-racialism," "constitutional freedom" and the like. Still, many well-meaning Americans adopt the concept of "color blindness" as a viable solution to our problems.

Michelle Alexander speaks quite eloquently to this issue:

> Few would openly argue that we should lock up millions of poor people just so that other people can have jobs or get a good return on their private investments. Instead, familiar arguments would likely resurface about the need to be 'tough' on criminals, not coddle them or give 'free passes.' The public debate would inevitably turn to race, even if no one was explicitly talking about it. As history has shown, the prevalence of powerful (unchallenged) racial stereotypes, together with widespread apprehension regarding major structural changes, would create a political environment in which implicit racial appeals could be employed, once again with great success. Failure to anticipate and preempt such appeals would set the stage for the same divide-and-conquer tactics that have reliably preserved racial hierarchy in the United States for centuries....Since the days of slavery, black men have been depicted and understood as criminals, and their criminal 'nature' has been among the justifications for every caste system to date. The criminalization and demonization of black men is one habit America seems unlikely to break without addressing head-on the racial dynamics that have given rise to successive caste systems. Although colorblind approaches to addressing the problems of poor people of color often seem pragmatic in the short run, in the long run they are counterproductive. Color blindness, though widely touted as the solution, is actually the problem." (239-240)

In a Stanford study, conducted in 2004, where the participants were police officers and undergraduate students, researchers investigated the influence of stereotyped associations on visual processing and found that when the faces of Black people were introduced, participants immediately perceived criminality and/or threat at a level that would impact their decisions and behavior (Eberhardt, Goff, Purdie, Davies; 2004).

We must deal with the problem of negative imagery head on. Whether it is represented by the crude dehumanizing nineteenth century imagery of Black citizens or the imagery of Jewish citizens produced by Nazi Germany, promotion of such imagery fuel the rationalization of scapegoating and prejudice that can lead to violence. Research indicates, for example, that in the south during the period between 1882 to 1930, whenever the price of cotton decreased, causing economic hardship, the lynching of Blacks by Whites increased (Hovland and Sears, 1940). More recently, negative imagery directed towards Muslims and Arabs have contributed to many devastating consequences at home and abroad (Jackson, 2013). The psychological impact of negative imagery is a therapeutic issue for all Americans regardless of skin color and there is no better place to start than with the media. It is a peculiar American export; homegrown and spread around the world.

"A nation which has made the despising of blacks a unique element of its identity is at a profound disadvantage when called upon to lock arms with people of other lands and form a brotherhood of nations." (Grier & Cobbs 1968, 30).

Today's youth are truly a generation of people impacted by the media. The images promoted through the audio, visual, and print media shape ideas about what to wear, what to say, how to act, and even *what* to think. Today's generation of young people, whether claiming membership in the hip hop generation or generation Xers, are accustomed to quick-paced, thrill-based, entertaining modes of obtaining information. This, of course, can be seen in the evident fervor for smaller and smaller devices that run on faster and faster networks. Once the announcement goes out for the new "iPad" (just to name a device, but it could be any of the next must-have devices, iPhone, Android etc..) the clamor is on; the lines begin with would-be customers camping outside the store the night before…to be the first of the firsts.

The thing of it is…whereas the technology has changed tremendously in the last one hundred years, the basic messages and images about Black people in general, and Black males in particular, have undergone relatively little change since the first Hollywood blockbuster, D.W. Griffith's *The Birth of a Nation*. Griffith was an ex-college roomate of President Woodrow Wilson (who thought the film was a landmark achievement) and his film was arguably one of the most racist films of all time, with its depiction of KKK members as national heroes beating back the terrifying hoards of newly emancipated savages. Of course the "virtue" of the white woman was at stake as was the fate of the country. If anything, the erroneous and false ideas have become more entrenched with the use of better technology. In Marlon Rigg's film, *Ethnic Notions*, (skillfully and beautifully narrated by the late Esther Rolle) we see the convenient and racist caricatures of black men and women. Europeans and white Americans found the need to characterize black women as the "mammy", an asexual typically overweight nurturer to the slave-master's family (at the expense of her own) and the "sapphire," a hypersexual, sassy and manipulative counterpart to the mammie. The black man was characterized by two dominant stereotypes. "Sambo" was used to promote the idea of the happy-go-lucky, lazy, good-for-nothing black man, "with an ear for music and an appetite for pork chops" as illustrated in Rigg's caption of the film *Rhapsody in Black and Blue* (1932).

Asante Jr. (2008) in his acclaimed work, *Its Bigger Than Hip Hop; The Rise of The Post Hip Hop Generation* discusses the notion that many in the post-hip-hop generation recognize that one of the most pervasive but seldom indentified forms of racism—one that "cuts across geographic, gender, age and class lines" is representation by way of mass media. The idea that regardless of political and educational progress, African-Americans have made very little headway in the area of mass media representation is one shared by my many social historians. These negative images have been stable and have devastating consequences for Blacks in general and Black youth in particular. Asante Jr. expands on these caricatures…

> …images of people of African descent remain virtually unchanged from the racist stereotypes promoted before and during slavery. Although there have been minor updates to the Black shadow cast on screen, the formula has remained fixed. Fixed, for the Black woman, has been Jezebel, the lewd mulatto; Sapphire, the evil, sex-crazed manipulative bitch; and Mammy, the Aunt Jemima nurturer whose sexuality has been so removed that she is best portrayed by Martin Lawrence (Big Momma's House), Tyler Perry (Diary of a Mad Black Woman), or Eddie Murphy (Norbit). For the Black man, fixed has been Bigger Thomas, the white-woman-crazed brute; Jack Johnson, the hyper-sexed, hyper-athletic super thug; and Uncle Tom, the asexual sidekick. (17)

Just as devastating to the American psyche was the stereotype used to demean the African man who dared to learn to read, to become educated and prolific in the English tongue, the caricature of "Zip Coon." "Zip Coon" became the ideal for the stumbling, bumbling, laughable character who utilized misplaced and created vocabulary quite to the amusement of white folk and carried the pretense of being "civilized" and educated. This caricature was no doubt created to help whites psychologically cope with the likes of men like Olaudah Equiano, Benjamin Banneker, Henry Highland Garnett and Frederick Douglas whose brilliant and fiery command of the English language put many of them to shame and sent fear throughout communities of white folk.

In 1852 Douglas was asked to speak at a 4th of July rally, which he did (Douglas; 2006). He famously asked the question "What to the American slave is your 4th of July?" and ferociously answered:

> I answer: a day that reveals to him, more than all other days in the year, the gross injustice and cruelty to which he is the constant victim. To him, your celebration is a sham; your boasted liberty, an unholy license; your national greatness, swelling vanity; your sounds of rejoicing are empty and heartless; your denunciation of tyrants, brass-fronted impudence; your shouts of liberty and equality, hollow mockery; your prayers and hymns, your sermons and thanksgivings, with all your religious parade, and solemnity, are, to him, mere bombast, fraud, deception, impiety, and hypocrisy—a thin veil to cover up crimes which would disgrace a nation of savages. There is not a nation on the earth guilty of practices more shocking and bloody than are the people of these United States, at this very hour.
>
> Go where you may, search where you will, roam through all the monarchies and despotisms of the Old World, travel through South America, search out

every abuse, and when you have found the last, lay your facts by the side of the
everyday practices of this nation, and you will say with me, that, for revolting
barbarity and shameless hypocrisy, America reigns without a rival. (p. 23)

One must wonder what it must have been like to hear such force and absolute
certainty from the mouth of a former slave. It is no wonder that white America, in order to deal with the very real anxiety that would emerge in the face of
such a stark challenge to their delusions about themselves and the slave class,
would create mental structures that would provide comfort and reassurance.
Reassurance of their place in the world juxtaposed to "inferior" blacks
whether slave or free, including their beliefs about the egalitarian nature of
life within the United States.

One writer, upon reading an article out of the *New York Times* entitled,
"The Self Destruction of the 1 Percent," that appeared in October 2012
explained that one statement in particular by the author (Chrystia Freeland)
almost forced the coffee from his mouth in revulsion.

I open the pages of the Sunday New York Times about two weeks ago to find
this remarkable sentence:
"In the early 19th century, the United States was one of the most egalitarian
societies on the planet."

This statement—bold and brash—appears in an essay "The Self Destruction of
the 1 Percent," by Chrystia Freeland, in the *New York Times* Sunday Review,
October 14…And I go: "What The Fuck!"
What about the slavery of Black people, at its peak—or its worst, depending
on your point of view—in that time period? What about the genocide of Native
peoples? Are they invisible, less than human? There is no mention of any of
this in the article.

Now, it is bad enough for Freeland to write this—it's a whole other thing for
the *New York Times*, America's "paper of record," to voice and propagate
this—without qualification, comment, or edit. Did the—vast—editorial apparatus of the NY Times not bat an eye at this statement? Is this how normalized
white-supremacist "white"-wash and amnesia of history is in so-called "en-
lightened" society? Or, rather, is this a Founding Myth (i.e.: LIE) and Grand
Narrative of America that the NY Times consciously and actively is working
to propagate?

Imagine a scenario in which a contributing author made the statement "Life
under the Nazis was a pleasant affair"—without sarcasm, irony, qualification,
comment or edit. One would be indignant and respond, "Not for the Jewish
people, who had a horrific Holocaust committed against them! Or the commu-
nists, gays and lesbians, other 'non-Aryan' nationalities"—and one would be
right and righteous in doing so. "Life under the Nazis was a pleasant affair":

Does one think this statement would pass the editorial muster of the New York Times Sunday Review ? November 4, 2012 | Revolution Newspaper

Our outraged commentator does have a point. Although Ms. Freeland writes what I feel is a wonderful comparative analysis of the Venetian Serrata and the *Serrata like* America of today, the piece does assume a sort of blindness to the reality of millions of non-European people. Ms. Freeland makes some extremely valuable points as she speaks to the growing educational chasm between the those at the top of our society and everyone else, the plutocratian think-tanks that have been financed towards the goal of weakening labor unions, and the knack the uber rich, "those at the tippy top of the economic pyramid," have for being very effective at capturing government support while "getting others to pay for it" (i.e., the 700 billion bail out of Wall Street in 2008, 93% of economic gains in 2009-10 going to the top 1%, of the 400 richest taxpayers—six paid no federal taxes; twenty-seven paid 10% or less; all paid no more than 35%). However, the following statement (to which our enraged writer above was referring) does reflect a type of obliviousness that many Black Americans would find offensive:

> In the early 19th century, the United States was one of the most egalitarian societies on the planet. "We have no paupers," Thomas Jefferson boasted in an 1814 letter. "The great mass of our population is of laborers; our rich, who can live without labor, either manual or professional, being few, and of moderate wealth. Most of the laboring class possess property, cultivate their own lands, have families, and from the demand for their labor are enabled to exact from the rich and the competent such prices as enable them to be fed abundantly, clothed above mere decency, to labor moderately and raise their families." (*New York Times*, "The Self Destruction of the 1 Percent" p. 5).

Certainly, given the bigotry and outright racism Thomas Jefferson openly expressed, it would come to no surprise that this would be his perspective on "greatness" of the United States of his time. But even in the context of a fine socio-economic and historical piece as this New York Times article, we should reasonably expect an editorial note (a nod, if you will) to those who, based on a different reading of the historical record, might not feel *all-too-egalitarian* about nineteenth century America.

K. K. Kambon (2006) in his discussion on the nature of definitional systems offers a useful framework for understanding such omissions. He states that we acquire our definitions via our sociocultural indoctrination. One's definitions constitute a shared phenomenon in that they embody an institutionalized process. They, in other words, represent the normative beliefs and attitudes of a social system. Definitions dictate the meanings we attach to events we experience in our everyday lives. Our definitions determine whether an event is considered important or unimportant, good or bad, factual or fictitious. In fact, our definitional systems supported by our predisposed attitudes and beliefs about the nature of life and existence helps determine whether or not we attend to an event at all. Thus, according to Kambon:

> In its most basic function, a definitional system prelimits the conceptual range of meanings that members of a social system will ultimately attribute to their experiences. This occurs primarily because definitions create in the individual a type of "perceptual set" or cognitive-emotional predisposition to experience events in a characteristic manner. Being an institutionalized process means that the influence of a definitional system is so thoroughly pervasive and subtle that prescriptions of the definitional system are simply experiences that members of the social system take for granted through their habitual or customary operation is accordance with them. The definitional system then dictates the normative way of thinking, feeling, and acting for those indigenous members of the social system. (58)

It is difficult to argue against the historic evidence revealing that throughout the world, wherever Europeans have encountered non-Europeans, they have fought vigorously, to militarily control the social space for themselves. Military effort has preceded ensuing attempts to gain psychological control over the social space by forcing the legitimacy of the European definitional system onto the non-European groups; providing Europeans determine the group has some functional value to their design. If not, the outcome has been total elimination of the non-European group.

In this context, one can see how Ms. Freeland and the editors of the *New York Times* might *miss* this very different perspective on the period. American historiography provides a basis for crafting mental structures that provide comfort and reassurance to white America about their place in the world. The above-stated article provides an example of media as institutional support for such delusions of grandeur. Often times, these statements go unquestioned.

One need only search the Internet to find every known stereotype about Black people in full view. At our fingertips are some of the most vile, vitriolic and racist websites and webpages in modern history. The Simon Wiesenthal Center publishes a list and sampling of various Neo Nazi/anti-Black websites.

Of great importance are the mental, emotional and behavioral consequences that emerge in a population as a consequence of surviving in such an insane environment. Although the sociological and psychological literature is repleat with deficiency-based explanations for the behavior (i.e., deviant behavior etc...) of Black people (Parham and White, 2000; Guthrie, 1998; Wilson, 1993) the fact is that rarely in this literature is it overtly stated that White middle-class people are being used as a measure for all people.

Rarely do we take the time to stop, step back and step out of what we consider our "normal" minds for a moment and look at the madness that exists all around us, let alone the madness we have existed in as a people. Who really has the time in this constantly buzzing and moving society. We would certainly do well to reconsider the White american collective community as a standard for comparison.

Amos Wilson in his discussion of "Insanity as a Model of Sanity" makes a most compelling argument:

> The most insane people on the earth today are used as models for sanity. The sanity of the racist European itself is not questioned. The insanity of European normality is not questioned. The possibility that what we call *normal* is itself *insane* is not questioned; that the organization of this society, the nature of its human relations, the structure of its economic systems, the values that motivate it, are the result of the madness of a people. (70)

Amos Wilson lays much of the responsibility for transmitting the kind of false realities that keep Black people in a state of frustration and dissatisfaction at the feet of the advertising industry; especially television advertising. Not only has traditional television advertising been designed to inculcate in Black people, a sense of inferiority but it diverts us from facing reality and confronting the truth of the "pitifulness" of our situatuion. Perhaps the one redeeming quality of "Reality TV" is that it has allowed Americans to see just how crazy some white families are rather than only presenting the *Leave it to Beaver* or *Father Knows Best* versions of White America!

When it comes to the normality and abnormality of Black consciousness and behavior as "politically mandated and socially manufactured by the power relations of White supremacy," Wilson believes they are characterized by the importance of certain disturbances of thought, emotions, motivations and values. These disturbances drive behavior and serve the interests of White hegemony. They do so by making Blacks highly reactive to social controls instigated by the White power structure.

These disturbances of thought, motivation, emotions and values which, in Blacks, are instigated and maintained by the White supremacist establishment for the purpose of sustaining its "normal" social order and relations are, according to Wilson, referred to as "pathological normalcy." If such thinking, values and motivated behavior were exhibited by Whites, these symptoms would be immediately considered "mental disorders" by the White mental health establishment. Amos Wilson clarifies that, "Pathological normalcy in Blacks refers to those disturbances in Black consciousness and behavior which are beneficial to the needs of Whites and to the perpetuation of White supremacy while being ultimately inimical to their own needs and liberation."

Symptoms of Thought Disturbance Include Amnesia and Delusions

Amnesia implies a total or partial loss of memory. It is a dissociative reaction occuring when an individual represses from consciousness, entire periods or episodes in his/her life and can result in the loss of pre-trauma identity. As stated in the previous chapter, "erasure of African memory" was a requirement for domination. The eradication of African cultural/historical memory was done to make possible the social manufacturing of the former African identity in a way that allows for its shaping and molding to fit the ongoing needs and interests of White supremacy. This means that the oppression of Blacks by Whites depends on the ability of Whites to create and maintain an ongoing descrepancy between what *subordinate* Africans "think they were and what they truly were; what they percieve themselves to be and what they truly are; what they think they should be and what they must be."

Through its ability to control avenues of communication and flow of information and through the its power to define reality the White supremacist structure has historically excluded the truth and true beauty of African history and culture from its own people and from the consciousness of Black/African people as a whole. Thus these powerful institutions of hegemony have been successful at associating the history and culture of Africans with feelings of shame, guilt and anxiety. Black people have historically suffered social ridicule, mental and physical abuse and experienced fear of social disapproval and humiliation to the extent that many have repressed and rejected the search for discovery of themselves.

Unfortunately this level of generational social amnesia prevents the discovery and reclamation of true African identity and prevents the discovery and exposure of true culture of White supremecy and of those who perpetrate it. In a last note on social amnesia Amos Wilson leaves us with a strong conundrum in consideration of the subordinate African...

> ...the reinforced social amnesia...permits him to...be just like; to identify with the captors, torturers, enslavers, lynchers and race-baiting sadistic exploiters of his ancestors and of himself...In his 'sweet' forgetfulness he is no longer motiviated to seek revenge, reparation, restitution, or reconstruction for past and present wrongs perpetrated by his White oppressors; he is not motivated to construct a new, Afrikan centered, humane utopia on the shattered remains of White supremacy's evil empire but to become an equal partner in it...thus sanctioning the annihilation of the personhood of both his ancestors and himself...Thus the subordinated Afrikan does not indict the supremacist regime for its misdeeds and require it to atone for its sins. Its constituents are left blameless and guiltless—having committed the *perfect crime* against Black humanity. These are but some of the benefits to White supremacy afforded by Afikan amnesia. (124-125)

Delusions can be seen as fixed false beliefs. They reflect beliefs that are ardently maintained and often defended despite being at odds with accepted reality, being inconsistent with logic and despite evidence to the contrary. Delusional individuals or groups maintain their beliefs even in the face of negative consequences that result from those beliefs being held.

The resulting *pathologically normal* behavior in subordinated Afrikans can be seen as directly connected to the White dominant power structure having the wherewithal to manipulate and, at times create, powerful cultural images, ideas, information, symbols, rewards and punishments and by way of their overwhelming social power, control social communication and interactions. By doing so, they inculcate subordinate Afrikans with delusions that are adverse in nature (acceptance of the non-African-ness of Mary/Mariam— mother of Jesus/Issa) and that drive attitudes and behaviors that advance the interests of White supremacy.

One need only discover the vast array of historical/cultural articles locked away in repositories around the world (including the Vatican) as confirmation of the European's control of cultural images and information.

A consequence of being inundated with false images, information, values and ideas and of systemic social control over reward and punishment for the subordinated African, is that his/her evaluation of an ideology or value is not rooted in logic with respect to objective reality; nor is it rooted in considering the extent to which the value or ideology may equalize the power relations between Whites and Blacks. According to Wilson, the basis for the deleterious belief is "not truth but expediency—the measure of pain or pleasure its holding and expression may bring to its host." The basis for accepting or rejecting an idea "becomes its emotional consequences rather than its truth value."

Fantasy is the result; and a life lived-out in fantasy either quietly in the mind or by acting out in real life is a delusionary one. Reactionary fantasies provide substitutes for desires which cannot be gratified in actuality. A new sports car (BMW etc...) may feel powerful but it is not power, especially when the owner has no driveway (land) to park it in. The desire to be a "pimp" creates more than a few "wanna be pimps" in Black communities. The "pimp" is not powerful but lives and acts in a world that is a reactionary fantasy of power. His actions energize and support the oppressive regime (where true power is held) by maintaining the further oppression of his own people and by reinforcing the stereotype.

If Black young men are nurtured in an environment comprised of such negative stereotypes, and if the philosophical basis of racism prevents challenging the belief system that supports these stereotypes and false beliefs, then American society becomes a problem for Black men.

One of my colleagues and mentor Dr. Frank Jones has spent years in youth advocacy, serving on several boards and as Professor of English Literature. In his work, *What Have We Done To Our Children—Positioning Black Children For Success* (2007), he discusses how most Black students in our school systems are treated by some "educators" as if they are dangerous and threatening to the well being of the instructor and to the institution. He tells the story of how a teacher in an Oakland, California middle school actually phoned the FBI to report that a young Black student in a classroom discussion said, "Bush needs to be whacked. I'll whack him!" Anyone who knows middle school students would understand that this was simply youthful bravado and ignorance...the kind of "trash talk" typical of powerless youths. But this instructor felt the child's statement warranted immediate action. She failed to call the principal. She failed to call the superintendent. She failed to phone any other official in the school district. She called the FBI directly and reported a threat against Bush's life. Her behavior and perception of a danger posed by that very young child to President Bush clearly was not connected to the reality or likelihood of the danger ever occurring.

Considering the inculcation of negative images within American society and the resulting behavior and orientation toward Black youth, Dr. Jones offers the following perspective in regard to black parenting:

> "James Baldwin once said—*if a Black person in America is not a little bit paranoid, he is a big bit crazy.* We have no reason, even today, to think that justice will run down like a mighty flood upon us. The systems of aggression have not been removed or torn down in any large measure. Instead, this society has retrenched into its old ways and has used surrogate Blacks to assist in their effort, viz., the Ward Connerlys of America...It is parenting that should be used as a result of the harsh American environment that our young Black males must grow up in...Beside the Horatio Alger ethic there is a philosophy peculiar to Black parenting: most Black parents teach their chidren the ABC's of relating to the police departments of America and the institutions of this society. And those ABC's are not the same as those taught by White parents...Black parents teach their male children that they should try to have as little contact with the police as possible...the police are hostile to Blacks' interests, well being, and often they are hostile to Black males' lives...Along with these admonitions...is another warning:the systems of society—public school, social services, etc.—are hostile to him, do not care for him, do not respect him, and if he is to succeed in these institutions he must be twice as smart or as qualified as his White counterparts." (Jones 2007, 69-71)

Given the media's power and the incredible wealth it has generated from Hip-Hop music and culture, its use could be revisited and its role in perpetuating negative myths about Black males should be considered in investigating solutions for the apparent problems.

Chapter Four

Research on Effects of Violence

Out of the body of research on violence, *five major conceptual frameworks* have developed to explain the types of effects caused by violence and traumatic events (Isaacs, 1992). *The victimization experience symptomatology* (Gordon, 1992) framework describes the linkages between characteristics of the experience of violence and individual symptomatology. The *stress and coping* framework attempts to explain the variability in effect of events, as due to the characteristics and intensity of stress, the individual's coping response, and individual differences in vulnerability or resilience. It is important to note that, under this framework, the intensity of the stressful events, the resulting psychic disequilibrium, and the success of the individual's coping mechanisms, determines what impact the stressful events will have on the individual's functioning. The *developmental framework* attempts to explain both short-term and long-term effects of traumatic events on children in terms of developmental characteristics or psychosocial stages. It also attempts to determine the impact of earlier traumatic events on functioning at later developmental stages. The *traumatic response framework* attempts to explain the effects of intensely aversive events, or events that seem to overwhelm most individual's coping capacities. This framework looks especially at studies of post-traumatic stress disorder (PTSD), many of which include combat veterans and rape victims. Studies have shown that many children who are victims of war or community violence suffer from PTSD related symptomatology. Acute stress disorder (ASD) could be included in this framework. The only distinction the DSM-5 makes in determining ASD from PTSD is onset and duration. ASD is diagnosed in cases where symptoms occur immediately or soon after the traumatic event and last for one month. In PTSD the symptoms continue longer than one month and can emerge shortly after the trauma or months or even years afterward. Symptoms generally include:

- Re-experiencing the traumatic event (recurring thoughts, flashbacks, dreams or nightmares).
- Avoidance behaviors of activities or any stimuli that elicit fear and that are connected to the traumatic event (including avoiding thoughts, feelings or conversations).
- Reduced responsivity (feeling detached from other people, dissociation or psychological separation; memory problems and a sense of derealization).
- Increased physiological arousal, negative emotions and guilt (hyper-vigilance, trouble concentrating, easily startled, sleep problems; also possible displays of anxiety, anger, depression or feelings of guilt).

Lastly, the *ecological* (Gordon, 1992) framework attempts to place stressful or traumatic events and their impact within higher order social contexts and to understand their effects within such contexts. Studies of the individual experience within the social ecological context include looking at family systems, community, and cultural context. A socio-ecological approach sets the stage for investigating the impact of community violence on African-American children and youth. An ecological model considers the history of violence in America, including the impact of violence on African-Americans during slavery, and the cultural context, which includes how norms, belief systems, and values are shaped. It also includes the historical, political, social, and economical realities that influence the social context and which compromise and, in some cases, determines the quality of life for many African-American children.

Certainly, the argument can be made for all frameworks being relevant to Black community members. When we consider the historic, multi-generational, four hundred plus years of violence perpetrated on African-descended people within the United States and other areas (the MAAFA) as well as the ongoing and systemic nature of violence perpetrated on Black people today, it is understandable how deep and complex the injury/injuries may be. Black people have experienced a type of PTSD connected to their unique and brutal circumstances here, in the United States and abroad. Several experts have considered the role of Post Traumatic *Slave* Disorder (PTSD) in understanding Black behavior today (Akbar, 1985; Hilliard, 1995; Kunjufu, 2004).

When in Bellevue, Washington, attending a conference of black educators and administrators, I was treated to a presentation by Dr. DeGruy-Leary, who has done pivotal work on the concept, "Post Traumatic Slave Syndrome" and whose most recently published book bears the same title. As a member of the audience, I was pleased when she used the analogy of arbitrarily shooting someone in the audience. She went on to explain that if she did this, the victim of the shooting would surely be severely traumatized. A member of the audience seated a few rows away might be traumatized and so might someone walking in the hallway who heard the gunshot. Further, the victim's family members who were never there to witness the shooting would, quite reasonably, be traumatized. However, someone in the audience who witnessed the shooting might not experience any symptoms of trauma, given the differences in reactivity human beings bring to the table.

She went on to argue that the person directly involved in the traumatic event, some of the people witnessing the event, those who never saw the event but heard the gunshot and those family members of the victim who never heard nor saw the event but who are affected by it by virtue of their relationship to the victim all may be candidates for therapeutic intervention having experienced a sufficient level of trauma to warrant the diagnosis of Post-Traumatic Stress Disorder (PTSD). This of course would depend on a variety of host-related factors (i.e. what each person brings to the table relative to how they deal with trauma).

In her book, Dr. DeGruy-Leary goes on to list the some of the conditions that may lead to mental and/or emotional traumas that justify the diagnosis of PTSD:

- A serious threat or harm to one's life or physical integrity
- A threat or harm to one's children, spouse or close relative
- Sudden destruction of one's home or community
- Seeing another person injured or killed as a result of accident or physical violence
- Learning about a serious threat to a relative or a close friend being kidnapped, tortured or killed.
- Stressor is experienced with intense fear, terror and helplessness
- Stressor and disorder is considered to be more serious and will last longer when the stressor is of a human design (p.118)

Then she asks the critical question: If the DSM (Diagnostic Statistical Manual) states that any one of these stressors is enough to cause PTSD, what about the African slaves who experienced ALL of them; many who were subjected to these traumatic experiences over and over again? Certainly they must have experienced PTSD. For those who experienced a lifetime of slavery and who watched their parents live and die under the cruelty of slavery, there were no counseling centers. There were no trauma centers when slavery ended in 1865. The trauma, quite simply was not only never addressed but it continued as stated in the previous chapters.

As mentioned earlier, the subjugation and subordination that defined chattel slavery included both a physical and mental processes. The success of the European slavery system depended on the destruction of the most essential aspect of African culture, African familial relationships. "If you were going to devise a uniquely cruel system of punishment, you could never have devised something more devastating and insidious than American chattel slavery because it absolutely, categorically destroyed existing relationships and undermined a people's ability to form healthy new ones" (DeGruy-Leary, p. 120).

Finally, DeGruy-Leary discusses how the effects of trauma are transmitted generationally through the process of parenting and highlights three important outcomes of generational trauma stemming from the slave experience; a debilitating belief in one's own inadequacy and sense of agency, vacant esteem and ever present anger. She argues that mostly when people discuss level of self-esteem in terms of high/low they are referring to matters of self-confidence and efficacy but that self-esteem has more to do with our sense of worth and value to our family, friends and larger community. As such, she defines vacant esteem as "the state of believing oneself to have little or no worth, exacerbated by the group and societal pronouncement of inferiority."

Although the concept of vacant esteem fits the victimization experience symptomatology framework it certainly could be seen as an ecological construct in that it is the result of three domains of influence—the society we live in including its constituent institutions, our community (we all-to-often, must survive) and our family.

Some of the symptoms of trauma Kunjufu (2004) cites include the following:

- A state of anxiety, dissatisfaction, or restlessness
- Chronic suicidal preoccupation
- Self-injury
- Explosive or extremely inhibited anger
- Compulsive or extremely inhibited sexuality
- Sense of helplessness or paralysis of initiative
- Shame, guilt or self-blame
- Sense of defilement or stigma
- Preoccupation with relationships with perpetrators
- Unrealistic attribution of total power to perpetrator
- Disruption of intimate relationships
- Isolation and withdrawal/ Sense of hopelessness and despair (p. 142-143)

Clearly, these symptoms can be observed in the lives of many members of Black communities in the United States and across the African diaspora; especially among communities plagued with violence.

It follows that prevention and treatment methodologies for victims of violence could benefit from the incorporation of all five conceptual frameworks. Within the context of these frameworks one can acknowledge that even perpetrators of violence are victims in a larger, more encompassing sense in that the mechanistic and materialistic narrative and worldview they operate from disconnects them from their own humanity. The constant need to control rather than partner with a world that is overwhelmingly people of color stems from a deep-seeded fear and subsequently an overwhelming compensatory need to appear fearless. In the process, generations of children are harmed while the perpetrators and stewards of such a historically violent, racially biased and economically unfair system must continue to build and/or support structures of denial thereby distancing themselves from their own sense of being. Violence can also be seen as cyclic with implications for attention and treatment at all levels.

PSYCHOLOGICAL IMPACT OF VIOLENCE

Black young men are almost inevitably victims of poverty, parental neglect, and abuse, systemic educational neglect leading to school failure, societal discrimination, and racism. Thousands of them are arrested and incarcerated each year without the benefit of appropriate psychological or psychiatric evaluation. Many more experience violence and loss of close friends and family members under the assumption of normality depending what they look like and where they live. Therefore, these youth receive no therapeutic treatment and no psychological assistance in helping them to resolve long-standing emotional conflict and psychological distress. The issues of frustration and anger are never addressed, and the resulting depression becomes entrenched and externalized.

It hadn't been quite a week yet after Michael (discussed in the intro) had been shot and killed when all of us from the block (my brother, my friends and I) were kicking back in the garage of one of our friends. The stand-alone garage was in the back towards the end of the driveway. We had all tricked our garages out back then with black light posters and cool colored lights and whatever stereo components we could throw together. Sometimes we would just connect a car stereo to an auto battery and trip-light speakers we had created. Whatever the case, it was our spot.

I can remember our going through the events of the shooting. We were simply trying to process a very traumatic event in our lives. We all liked Mike. He was our friend… our "dog"… and we were going to miss him. We were all still in disbelief that Mike was gone and we were concerned about his family, especially his little brothers. Mike didn't appear to have beef with shooters. We were trying to figure out the perennial question… why? As we were talking things over we noticed sounds outside the garage. They were subtle sounds. As we moved to check it out we noticed movement as we could see in areas where there was space between the exterior wood panels. We could tell someone was moving outside and instantly we knew they were police. Once we got out of the garage to confront them, as it became apparent they were spying on us, they attempted to question us. They wanted to know if we were planning on retaliation. Obviously nothing that they heard while eavesdropping confirmed their opinion.

They frisked us…guns at the ready under blinding flashlights. Of course nothing was found and they were on their way. It wasn't until many years later that I contemplated the fact that rather than to offer any type of support (mental health or otherwise) to several young men who had just experienced a huge and shocking loss, the police were there with the hopes of arresting some or all of us. They didn't care about Mike…and they didn't consider us as having human feelings of grief.

Thirty plus years later, Oscar Grant's friends would receive no more support from the police apparatus than we did. We were never asked by anyone if we wanted or needed counseling. The mental health "community" did not come to our aid. Nothing. Nothing for us…nothing for Oscar's friends, in terms of investment in their mental health as victims of trauma. No investment in our human-ness. The criminal "justice" system does however invest heavily in numbers and statistics.

Statistics on crime are only concrete indicators of the extent of criminal behavior; they provide no information on the psychological factors underlying such destructive behavior, nor do they provide insight into the more subjective aspects of this behavior. In consideration of underlying psychological social issues, again, Jewell Gibbs (1988) offers that delinquent and criminal behavior for psychologically disturbed young Black males can be viewed as serving two functions. The first being that this group of young men have not developed intra-psychic controls which enable them to moderate their impulses, to delay gratification of immediate needs, or to anticipate the consequences of their actions. The second function has to do with the anger and rage they carry, which results from the accumulation of years of frustration over their own victimization. Their anger and rage is displaced onto this society, which has been unable, or *unwilling* (emphasis mine) to protect and nurture them.

The devaluing of Black life and the mentality of self-hatred among many people of African descent are two factors that have had tremendous impact on violent outcome among Black males today (Hammond & Yung, 1993; Poussaint, 1972). Today's violence in African-American communities is seen, by some, as a direct result of psychological oppression of African Americans by the White power structure (Harvey, 1989; Gibbs, 1988; De-Gruy-Leary, 2012). After centuries of neglect and varying levels of abuse and abandonment, many African Americans have internalized the myths of Africans having no culture, no valid civilizations, and no high learning or scientific endeavor. Faulty compensatory attempts, such as identifying with the oppressor, have led to self-alienation and to a blocking of developmental stage transitions, leading to feelings of hopelessness and helplessness, which combine to equal perceived powerlessness (Harvey, 1989). Perceived powerlessness can be seen as a precursor to two primary emotions: depression and anger. Depression has been defined as an internalized expression of perceived powerlessness whereas anger is defined as an externalized expression of perceived powerlessness. In the state of depression we see individuals, families, and communities that elicit self-destructive behavior such as alienation, acting out, drug abuse, alcoholism, and prostitution. These acts can be seen as forms of slow suicide. In the externalized state of anger or rage, which usually results in homicide, the anger is acted out upon that which is closest or most convenient and on that which will minimize retribution from larger society. Historically we have seen that this often means murder of another African-American. In his book *Black-on-Black Violence: The Psychodynamics of Black Self-Annihilation in Service of White Domination,* Amos Wilson (1990) adds another dimension to the discussion of White supremacy and its outgrowth of racism and oppression as the primary causal factor in violence and criminality among African Americans. He states that "Black-on-Black homicide is a direct result of Black men not yet choosing to challenge and neutralize, on every front, the widespread power of White men to rule over their lives" (xiii). He also sees Black-on-Black violence as a natural outcome of continued White oppression and focuses on the fact that unemployment, poverty, lack of education, drugs, etc., which are often cited as causal factors are related to Black-on-Black violence, but represent secondary effects rather than causes. Dr. Akbar puts it a little differently. As he opens his book *Visions for Black Men* (1991), in chapter one, he explains that the full title of the chapter "From Maleness to Manhood" should be: "From Maleness to Manhood: The Transformation of the African-American Consciousness, or For Colored Boys Who Have Considered Homicide When Manhood Was Enough." What a wonderful title! If only the restrictions of space were not an issue and the intended youthful audience exercised the capacity to attend and comprehend it. Later on Dr. Akbar explains what many of us know all too well; the fact that the moment a Black (African) man stands up and declares himself to be a man, he has placed himself in absolute and immediate opposition to the European system, "which has defined him by their definitions as less than a man or as not a man."

On walls of apartment buildings, elevated subway stations, and malt liquor billboards, the C and B of Crips and Bloods were ubiquitous. Pint-sized gang-bangers, strapped, insecure, and terribly thin-skinned, perpetuated self-geno-cide with a ruthlessness too reminiscent of Rwanda. Though they shared the names of infamous South Central gangstas, the menace involved wasn't drive-

bys or the economic imperatives of crack-era cartels.... Some were as young
as ten and had the nasty intelligence of the kids from Brazil's *City of God*, with
whom they shared dismal prospects and the same desire for validation. (Nelson George, *The Plot against Hip-Hop*)

The problem of teen violence within the Black community is, no doubt, a
multifaceted one. Research has shown that one of the leading risk factors for
violence is poverty and that the hopelessness and lack of life options that
accompany poverty contributes to low or vacant self-esteem and depression,
which in turn increases the risk of exposure to violence (Spivak et al., 1989).
In addition, anger associated with poverty and racism can lower a person's
threshold for violence (Akbar, 1980; Erickson, 1968). The level of psychic
stress young Black males experience on an everyday basis in our society can
also be seen as key to violent behavior among this group. Pierce's (1970)
explanation of the concept of micro-aggression is useful in understanding the
high level of psychic stress experienced by Black youth. For Black youth,
who grow up in the inner city, the city they call home is an extremely hostile
environment. These youth are presented with daily reminders of their "lowly" status in American society. These reminders come in various subtle and
blatant ways to a young Black male. For example, a teacher calls him stupid,
a White stranger gets up and walks away when he sits down next to him on a
crowded bus, a bank teller reacts with suspicion and goes beyond normal
verification procedures when he attempts to cash a check, an employer refuses to interview him for a job, a clerk ignores him in a department store or
a salesman follows him around suspiciously, a cab driver passes him by or
moves on to a Caucasian person awaiting a taxi, a police officer stops him
and questions him in a White neighborhood or harasses and arrests him for
no known or apparent reason. These examples of micro-assaults are so common that most Black youth learn unconsciously to anticipate such incidents.
Black youth also learn to ignore or discount racist incidents. Many of these
youth have fragile egos indicating low self-esteem and low frustration tolerance, rendering them unwilling or unable to delay reactions to such incidents.
Jewell Gibbs' (1988) exposé of Hobson's choice summarizes their dilemma
beautifully:

>...If they do not respond to the assaults and insults they may internalize their
>anger and become depressed, develop psychosomatic symptoms like hypertension and ulcers, or drown their frustrations in alcohol and drugs; if they do
>react in a confrontational way to these assaults their response might easily turn
>to uncontrolled aggression and lead to assaults and invite counter violence
>from the very people who insulted them in the first place. No matter what
>choice they make, these daily negative interactions take an enormous toll on
>the mental health of Black youth in America. (p. 242)

And the toll can also be measured in blood. What happened to Oscar Grant, Trayvon Martin, Jordan Davis, Michael Brown, Eric Garner, Kendrick Johnson (murdered and his body desecrated in Valdosta, Georgia) and a host of others stand as a testimony to what can happen to Black young men who pose no danger at all and what happened to them should not happen to anyone. From all over the country, millions of people raised their voices in dissent of what can be considered criminal negligence on behalf of the police departments involved in overseeing the investigation into the above murders. Although many called for peaceful protests and most of the protests were, in fact, peaceful, it wasn't until the police establishment felt the threat of the escalation of violent action that it got in motion and moved some of the murderers through the legal process. Even still, only one of the above cases has brought a conviction and no law enforcement perpetrator has been prosecuted to the extent of the law. This failure of the legal system to act when Black youth are victims of white shooters only adds to the psychosomatic illness Hobson describes above.

NEURO-PLASTICITY AND TRAUMA

We now know that these physical health consequences create a feedback loop affecting mental health and brain function. The role of trauma and stress in damaging critical brain structures (i.e., hippocampus, amygdala etc.) and in disrupting the essential HPA (Hypothalamic-Pituitary-Adrenal-Cortical-Axis) pathway, responsible for the ever-important balance between our fight or flight (sympathetic) and calming (parasympathetic) systems as well as regulation of the endocrine system are well documented.

The experience of multi-generational trauma and re-victimization by hostile system of jurisprudence helps create a host of health and mental health related complications in children and youth.

We understand that cognitively children's responses to violence reflect a conflict between cognitive evaluation of the violent event (their ability to understand the meaning of the event and the extent to which they feel personally threatened) and their resources for controlling emotions; that degree of disturbance in younger children is influenced by parental reaction to the event; and that children's reaction to events can differ depending on their age.

However, the health impact belies a mind/body connectedness with devastating multi-generational effects that go well beyond the transmission of unhealthy parental practices. There is a growing body of evidence that stress-related issues wreak havoc on our delicate brain-body biochemical relationship.

Consider the important roles of the hormones estrogen and testosterone. They are extremely important for brain health in that estrogen impacts serotonin receptors in males and females, estrogen impacts dopamine and acetylcholine receptors in females and testosterone impacts dopamine receptors in males. Healthy hormone levels have been shown to facilitate neuronal branching and plasticity, to slow brain degeneration and impede brain inflammation. The female frontal lobe has more receptor sites for estrogen and the male frontal lobe, more receptor sites for testosterone. It is not uncommon for a woman who presents with low estrogen to suffer from depression and lack of motivation and the same can be said for men with low testosterone levels.

Microglia cells also synthesize hormones but require precursors to do so. For example, they require cholesterol as well as DHEA (dehydroepiandrosterone). DHEA is made throughout the body but the majority is released from the adrenal glands. Stress can heavily impact adrenal function and poor adrenal function means low DHEA output. This is but one of many important relationships impacted by trauma and stress. They are critical biochemical relationships that are part of a sequelae of events connected to childhood experience of violence that appear to impact health throughout the life span.

In their longitudinally designed study on childhood trauma and telomere maintenance Shalev, Moffitt and Caspi (2012) looked at the notion that because stress in early life is known to have a direct effect on poor health later in life, focus on the underlying biological mechanisms through which children may acquire lasting vulnerability to disease may lie in changes to DNA. Consequently their focus was in line with the body of new research that suggests that stress exposures can accelerate the erosion of DNA segments known as telomeres. Specifically, the authors hypothesized that cumulative violence exposure would accelerate telomere erosion in children while they experienced stress. Previous studies have confirmed telomere erosion as measured by telomere length (TL) however it has not been clear whether telomeres began eroding during exposure to stress or many years later. What the authors found was that children who were physically maltreated showed significantly accelerated telomere erosion from age 5 to 10 and those children who experienced one or more kinds of violent exposure showed significant TL erosion compared to children who had one or no violent exposures even when adjusting for confounding variables.

In addition, this effect has been indicated in utero. Entringer (et al, 2012) in their research on prenatal programming of newborn and infant telomere length provided the first evidence in humans that nutrition and stress may exert a programming effect on the newborn and infant telomere biology system. Using cord blood for newborns and buccal cells for infants, they measured TL and concluded that differential exposures to stress in the critical period of birth could impact ensuing health and disease susceptibility over the life span, including aging and longevity.

> One-hundred and eighty years of the Middle Passage, 246 years of slavery, rape and abuse; one hundred years of illusory freedom. Black codes, convict leasing, Jim Crow, all codified by our national institutions. Lynching, medical experimentation, redlining, disenfranchisement, grossly unequal treatment in almost every aspect of our society, brutality at the hands of those charged with protecting and serving. Being undesirable strangers in the only land we know. During the three hundred and eighty-five years since the first of our ancestors were brought here against their will, we have barely had time to catch our collective breath. That we are here at all can be seen as a testament to our willpower, spiritual strength and resilience. However, three hundred and eighty-five years of physical, psychological and spiritual torture have left their mark. (DeGruy-Leary 111-112)

PTSD, ASD, PTSS, micro-aggressions, perceived powerlessness, oppressive institutions and the obfuscation of their existence converge to create a crisis in health and mental health for Black youth, of epidemic proportions. Part of what emerges from these set of experiences for Black youth are disruptions in mood, in modulation of anger when there are few constructive outlets for its expression and in the ability to deal with frustration in a productive manner. I refer to this triad as the Three Headed Dragon.

Chapter Five

The Three Headed Dragon: Frustration, Depression, and Anger Frustration

Another important aspect of this work will be the focus on the individual's ability to tolerate frustration. We have seen previously where frustration shares an intimate relationship with violent-assaultive behavior.

Frustration has long been regarded as a major instigation to anger and aggression. Discussions as to its associative nature and antecedent function to anger and aggression can be traced back to the early 1920's and to the likes of Mcdougall and Freud (Averill, 1982). Scientific theories in America on frustration date back to the early 1930's. Lawson (1965) categorized theories of frustration into either *self-contained theories* or *theories integrated with general behavior theory* (Amsel, 1992). He placed Rosenzweig's frustration theory (1934), Dollard, Doob, Miller, Mower, and Sears' frustration-aggression hypothesis (1939), Barker, Dembo, and Lewin's frustration-regression hypothesis (1941), and the frustration-fixation hypothesis (Maier, 1956) all in the category of self-contained theories because they identified the study of frustration as a topic in its own right.

Rosenzweig's theory was heuristic in nature and consisted of three major points. First, he developed a very general definition of frustration. He saw frustration as an occurrence of an obstacle that prevented the satisfaction of a need. Secondly, Rosenzweig developed a classification of types of reactions to frustration, including the concepts of extrapunitive, intropunitive, and impunitive reactions (Rosenzweig, 1934, 1938). Lastly, Rosenzweig investigated the concept of frustration tolerance. He offered that frustration tolerance tended to increase with age, and the idea that there is an optimal amount of frustration an individual should experience at certain developmental levels in order to eventually attain a maximum level of frustration tolerance. One outgrowth of Rosenzweig's work in frustration tolerance concerns memory and preference for success and failure experiences as a function of age (Rosenzweig, 1945). Rosenzweig regarded this as an indicator of frustration tolerance. He considered recall of or a tendency to resume tasks on which the subject had previously failed as indicating higher frustration tolerance. This seems reasonable in that it is necessary for young men to face and successfully meet social challenges to achieve social and emotional development. For this, frustration tolerance is requisite.

The frustration-aggression hypothesis advanced by Dollard et al. came out of Yale's Institute of Human Relations. The hypothesis was an attempt to formalize ideas that were to be found in the early writings of Freud. Dollard et al. proposed that the occurrence of frustration always increased the tendency for an aggressive response, and whenever an organism responded aggressively, this was, in effect, evidence of the previous state of frustration.

Barker et al. also formalized an earlier Freudian hypothesis seeking to create more objective terms suitable for experimentation. Freud suggested that frustration could cause one to revert to modes of behavior likened to those of an earlier developmental stage. This was the basis of the frustration-regression hypothesis. An outgrowth of this work was the formation of field theory. As in the case of Dollard et al.'s frustration-aggression hypothesis, the research done by Barker et al. was not without its flaws. However, among them we see the joint influence of Freud and commonsense ideas about frustration being presented in a more formal and testable fashion (Lawson, 1965).

Because Maier's frustration-fixation hypothesis was based on experimental work, his approach appeared rigorous and formal. However, it had elements in common with the earlier theories and, like the others, was influenced by a commonsense appraisal of frustration. Maier, contrary to the frustration-aggression hypothesis, stated that the characteristics of behavior in a frustrating situation was that it became *fixated*.

Maier's research was done primarily with rats. He achieved interesting results, out of which he developed a more operational definition of a frustration situation: one in which no adaptive, goal-oriented behavior can develop, but one in which the subject must continue to respond. After conditioning rats in an insoluble situation in one instance, Maier and his co-workers proceeded to compare the frustrated rats with normally-trained, rewarded rats (Maier, 1949). After both rats had developed a consistent stereotyped response to one window, that window was permanently locked and the opposite window permanently unlocked. Maier observed that all of the normally-trained rats would quickly abandon their formerly correct response and adopt the new one, but a large number of frustrated rats would not do so even after as many as 200 trials. Although in all trials the subjects were punished for incorrect responses, the frustrated rats did not deviate from their original stereotyped response. Maier saw this as fixation and believed that it could only be remedied by the technique of *guidance,* or gently forcing the rat to jump opposite to its fixated preference. The rigidity that results from unpredictable and uncontrollable situations could be an important facet of frustration for Black youth considering real life issues of nihilism, fatalism, and lethargy. When young Black men learn that no matter what they do their lives will still be subject to the same negative debilitating consequences, the result is hopelessness, helplessness and, as Maier put it, fixation.

Yates (1962) felt that Maier's work had been unjustifiably played down by American behavioral psychologists. The main reason for this seemed to be that Maier insisted that fixated behavior was controlled by principles other than those that formed the basis of general behavior theory.

Lawson identified the second category of theories as Child and Waterhouse's (1952) revision of the frustration-regression hypothesis, Brown and Farber's (1951) conceptualization of frustration as an emotion and an intervening variable, and Amsel's (1958) frustrative nonreward theory.

The distinguishing characteristics of such theories include their closer relationship to more formal behavior theory, marked by a more technical view of the concept of frustration. This second stage of theories carried over trends that were anticipated in the earlier set of theories. However, this new generation of theorists brought these trends closer to fruition. Lawson (1965) cites these trends:

> Distinguishing characteristics of this stage were: 1) An increasing emphasis on a wide variety of experimental work as the basis for theorizing as opposed to reliance on everyday examples of frustration and its effects . . . 2) Coupled with a broader experimental base, these theories also attempted a closer alliance with more formal behavior theory . . . 3) Instead of seeking a unique generic term or unique model for "frustrating situations," it came to be recognized that many kinds of already well-known independent variables could be involved . . . 4) This latter, trend, in turn, brought a growing suspicion that there was no unique overt behavior-characteristic of frustration situations. (p. 27)

Child and Waterhouse's (1952) main point was that to treat regression, or *lowered constructiveness of play,* as the primary outcome of frustration was to oversimplify the case. They believed that *lowered constructiveness* referred to some general characteristic of behavior as a whole, and that frustration probably could not have such a pervasive singular effect. Child and Waterhouse felt that when goal-directed behavior is in some way interfered with, motivation is changed and other responses are likely to occur. Further, they believed that the effect of motivational change can only be predicted by knowing a great deal about the behavioral options possible for a given subject in a given situation, and knowing the subject's past history.

Brown and Farber (1951) borrowed from Hullian theory in their treatment of emotions in general. They felt that frustration could be regarded as a higher-order hypothetical construct, and explored the possibility that frustration could be defined in terms of such constructs (higher-order constructs theoretically can be related directly to observables). Similar to Child and Waterhouse, they used the premise that when the tendency to perform a particular response is interfered with, other tendencies to respond are aroused by this interference. Therefore, Brown and Farber saw frustration as a conflict between two opposing response tendencies—one response tendency being the one originally evoked by the situation, and the other being some alternative response aroused by the frustration interfering conditions themselves.

Abram Amsel, influenced by the efforts of Brown and Farber, also used the hypothetical construct approach. However, his construct was different. Amsel's (1958) contribution to this line of thinking was to add the notion that nonreward caused a *frustration reaction,* and components of this reaction could likewise be conditioned to other stimuli in the environment. Amsel's contribution to the evolution of frustration theory is two-fold: (1) Only one basic operation is considered in this theory (nonreward after experience with reward), which is in contrast to some of the lists of variables that can lead to frustration put forth by earlier psychologists. (2) His anticipatory frustration concept is used to explain long-standing problems in the field of learning, namely, the effect of intermittent reinforcement on resistance to extinction, and the occurrence of discrimination learning. Amsel's (1992) work served to augment the developmental changes in the conceptualization of frustration. He, among others, was not concerned with the vernacular meaning of frustration. Consequently, in the area of research, the term *frustration* has taken on more restricted sets of generalizations.

Research has demonstrated that frustration is neither a necessary nor a sufficient condition for aggression. Therefore, it is doubtful that we would find a psychologist that subscribes to the frustration-aggression hypothesis in its original form. However, many theorists still see frustration as a major source of aggression, in that frustration often leads to anger and aggression is a common manifestation of anger. In fact, violence is usually a product of prolonged and severe frustration of any and all innate drives (Davies, 1989). Although frustration is one of the factors most frequently recognized as being involved in the instigation of anger (Averill, 1982), it is important to understand that the outcome may not necessarily always be aggression or aggressive behavior.

The Dictionary of Concepts in General Psychology (1988) describes frustration as connoting the thwarting that is experienced when activity that is considered to be important is interrupted. Amsel offers more detail in his explanation of primary, *unlearned* frustration as a "natural reaction of probably all higher animals to nonattainment of goals, to thwarting, and to en-countering physical or psychological barriers or deterrents in the path of goal attainment" (p. 43).

The state of frustration is of utmost importance to the understanding and treatment of young African-American males. The definition speaks to the actual condition of these young men. They are constantly confronted with the thwarting of aspirations and very basic desires (i.e., to be treated fairly and as human beings with the same right to opportunity in life as any other human being). They are reminded, on a daily basis, of their inequality in stature and of their "limited" potential in relationship to people of other ethnic back-grounds who are culturally intact and autonomous, or come from voluntary immigrant groups (Gibbs, 1988; Ogbu, 1987). This comes at a severe cost to their level of self-esteem. They experience a blocking of their ability to transition at each stage of development and are frustrated economically, po-litically, and socially within this society (Issacs, 1992). Many of these young men begin to internalize the myths and negative images of Blacks that ema-nate from and are supported by a sick and corrupt power structure, thereby increasing the level of frustration and self-alienation. This leads to feelings of hopelessness and helplessness, which, as stated earlier, are equivalent to perceived powerlessness (Harvey, 1992). An outcome of this process is the internalization of powerlessness, which, in part, leads to the primary emotion (or state) of depression.

American society reinforces frustration at every developmental turn for young African-American males. Considering this society's resistance to healing historical wounds, it is incumbent on those in the field of clinical psychology to research and develop methodology that will enhance the abil-ity of African-American males to tolerate and thrive in the midst of various levels of ongoing frustration. People who tolerate frustration understand and believe that their goals are attainable and are able to see the light at the end of the tunnel. Many young African-American males not only do not see the light at the end of the tunnel but fail to perceive the tunnel. Many have developed fatalistic and nihilistic attitudes in attempting to cope with their reality, which is paved with bitterness. Their spirit has been crushed. They do not know who they are and do not know from whence they've come. Al-though the above theorists eloquently and scientifically discuss the construct of frustration as it relates to aggression from an individual organismic level it can be argued, that they remain limited by their frame of reference. There is no place in the various models to discuss injury to one's spirit as a function of frustration nor do they contemplate the collective nature of frustration let alone the type of spiritual essence that could produce a level of frustration tolerance that would allow a people to survive and thrive; even in the absence of reward or any tangible outlets.

DEPRESSION

Depression has a profound impact on young African-American males, yet no culturally relevant psychological strategies have been developed to treat it. The symptomatology of depression runs the gamut from slow suicide and apathetic behavior to rampant fatalism and outright violent assault. Depression is not only the most frequent mental health problem in America, but it is also the most serious, exerting a multitude of effects at the biological level, the psychological level, and the familial level. It has been viewed as both an antecedent to violent behavior and a result of violent victimization.

Depression has been noted for thousands of years, with some reports dating as far back as biblical times. Theories of cause have varied from disturbances in body humors, to metaphysical causes, to the result of evil possessions, to moral weakness. Beck (1973) and Gilbert (1992) provide a detailed (although Eurocentric) history of the major theoretical and historical movements in the classification and defining of depression. Debate has surrounded three major areas of concern within the last century (Gilbert, 1992): (1) Is depression a dimensional variation from normal or something alien, abnormal, and a disease with its own autonomous action? (2) Can we study the biology of depression separately from psychological and social processes or can the psychological aspects of depression be studied with no regard to the biological basis of suffering and brain processes? and (3) Can we ignore that there are important implications for social power regardless of the approach we take? Gilbert (1992), in his book *Depression: The Evolution of Powerlessness*, makes an interesting case for approaching the problem of depression from a biopsychosocial perspective:

> While I have great respect for my biological colleagues it is quite untenable to believe that in the majority of these cases we are dealing with a disease and can now drug our way out of trouble. To advance our knowledge further, new ways must be found to develop multidisciplinary and biopsychosocial theories. If not we will end up with an ever-increasing number of theories, useless conflicts over whether depression is a disease or not. . . . More serious, prevention becomes a fragmented endeavor with different groups peddling different ideas, many of which fail to deal with our lifestyles as the problem for many. The importance of understanding the causes of depression as a multilevel phenomenon (genetic threshold, early family life, psychological styles and social context) can hardly be overstated. . . . In this book . . . [a]n endeavor is made to indicate how social and psychological processes influence biological processes by virtue of the evolutionary path we have journeyed. (p. 5)

Although he does not explicitly include the role of the Gut/Brain axis in his discussion on multi-disciplinary approaches, I'm sure Gilbert's perspective would leave room for the role of diet as part of the social context for depression. Ample evidence has been shown to indicate the important biochemical mechanisms (appropriate levels of the neurotransmitters serotonin, dopamine, epinephrine and norepinephrin; brain inflammation; hormonal levels etc...) involved in depression (Kharrazian, 2013). However, we will focus here on psychosocial contributions.

An important aspect to the discussion of approaches is the issue of power and the relationship of power to defining depression (Turner, 1987). The power to define the problem also means the power to define its boundaries and domains of expertise. This issue is important because the classification debates carry hidden agendas of who can do what to whom, how prevention programs should be organized, and how resources are allocated. All these debates carry with them ethical dilemmas (Canson, 1993). If any mental disorder is defined as a disease of the body, then it requires special knowledge of biological processes to treat it. This is of interest to major drug companies who, of course, have vested interests in biological treatments, and whose practices are questionable here in the United States as well as in third world countries. In many cases depression may represent a disturbance of biopsychosocial patterns of living (Gilbert, 1992), which leaves room for taking into consideration powerful social and sociopsychological factors in its treatment. Gilbert's point is well taken and quite relevant to the treatment of depression in American males of African descent, considering the long history of psychosocial and psychological insults many of them carry when presenting for treatment.

One important psychosocial factor relevant to depression, and one that impacts young African-American males on a daily and consistent basis, is the consequence of social ranking. Price (1989) pointed out that whereas there is increasing research into renal disorders, immunological deficiency, and cardiac disease, as a consequence of aggression down the hierarchy, psychopathologists have yet to engage in detailed and coherent psychobiological research studies of ranking stress. Ranking is, above all else, a means of deciding social control and preferential access to resources. Clearly, African-American males, and in particular young males, are at the subordinate end of this social ranking system. Subordinates occupying a low rank position have little social control over access to breeding resources, are tense and biologically stressed (Henry & Stephens, 1977; Sapolsky, 1989). Ranking is an important aspect of the study of treatment modalities for depression in young African-American males. Social ranking is woven into the fabric of this society on the basis of race and on the premise of White male supremacy. The fact that young African-American males are a direct threat to this paradigm by virtue of their very existence plays out clearly in such a system. Ranking behavior is an important dimension of human social life, covering a diversity of social concepts. It is implicit in the use of terms such as social power, dominance, status, respect, prestige, and authority, relative to individuals, groups, nations, or even objects (Clark, 1990; Gilbert, 1992). Gilbert makes a pungent point in relationship to social ranking and one that is of significance to the relevance and the complexity of depression in young African-American males:

> The common thread that runs through this diversity is that there is a natural tendency to understand, think about or construe relationships, between things, people and objects, in terms of some ranked relationship, and these construc-tions influence our attention and behavior towards them. In humans, ranks can arise from the power to move against others but also the ability to attract others and have social attention and status bestowed. (p. 150-151)

For the most part, the human acquisition of status is connected to the demon-stration of one's positive qualities (i.e., abilities, knowledge, beauty, etc.). If one considers the history of Blacks in America, one can appreciate the dif-fuse nature of the barriers to status and social ranking for African-American males. If we understand the history of racism and the negative images it has produced, its effect on African peoples across the diaspora, and its particular destructive effect on Africans in America, we can see that for young African-American males, the larger social structure is and has been a complex, de-pressive web—a system wherein the causes of depression and stress may not be so clear but are quite deadly. Price (1988) suggests that signals of social power can be classified in two ways. Signals that are emitted with the pur-pose of reducing rank/status or maintaining a conspecific in a subordinate position can be called catathetic signals. Catathetic signals involve various signals of threat, put-down, or non-recognition of another's attempts to achieve respect or status. Signals that boost status in others are anathetic signals. Anathetic signals can be involuntary, such as submissive signals, where receivers of submissive signals have their dominance and social power confirmed. The interaction between Black youth and the police in the United States can certainly be used as an example of the interplay between both anathetic and catathetic signals. The power structure is reinforced by way of heavy-handed tactics and use of threat and weaponry. It is also reinforced by submissive postures exhibited by citizens at the behest of the police or through conditioning. The "Stop and Frisk" program provides a perfect ex-ample of the abuse of such signals. The oppressive program had become just another fact of life under occupation for many youth in New York city. The Center for Constitutional Rights (2012) documented disturbing reports of children being stopped by police on their way to and from school. They were often lined up, holding the wall with legs spread while police went through their pockets.

> "When police come around, I make sure I keep my head down. I'm very cautious of where I go. Unfortunately, now I plan my destinations to a T."

—24 year old Black woman, Lower East Side

"It's the difference between frisking somebody and going in their underwear or like putting gloves on outside, checking other people's private areas, and people's rectal area... its just too much, outside—that's embarrassing."
—20 year old Black/Dominican man, Hamilton Heights

"My sister got kind of scared. She started crying. And then I felt kind of bad... so I started crying too. I was 12. They told me that if I don't stop crying, they're going to put me in cuffs and take me in too."
—16 year old Puerto Rican youth, Brooklyn
(CCR report; Stop and Frisk: the Human Impact)

Signals can also be voluntary, where the signals relate to various forms of respect, morale boosting, appreciation, and adulation. These signals occur, negatively or positively, on a daily basis and are an intricate piece to the complex matrix of attitudes, behavior, and social structures that result in the depressive symptomatology of young African-American males.

Depression can be seen as having two basic distinctions (Gilbert, 1992): (1) primary depression and (2) secondary depression. Primary depression may be unipolar or bipolar and is not preceded by any other psychiatric or physical disorder. Secondary depression is preceded by and may accompany other psychiatric disorders or a physical disorder. Beck (1976), defines depression in terms of the following attributes:

1. A specific alteration in mood: sadness, loneliness, apathy.
2. A negative self-concept associated with self-reproaches and self blame.
3. Regressive and self-punitive wishes: desires to escape, hide, or die.
4. Vegetative changes: anorexia, insomnia, loss of libido.
5. Change in activity level: retardation or agitation.

The symptomatology of depression can fall in any of six categories which include emotional manifestations, cognitive manifestations, motivational manifestations, vegetative and physical manifestations, delusions, and hallucinations (Beck, 1976). This work relative to depressive symptomatology focuses on the former three; emotional manifestations, cognitive manifestations, and motivational manifestations. These manifestations of depression seem to be closely related to violence and to violent victimization in the Black community and in young African-American males in particular (Issacs, 1992; Hill, 1992).

Emotional manifestations refer to the changes in a person's feelings or to the changes in his/her behavior directly attributable to his/her feeling states. Emotional manifestations include dejected mood, negative feelings toward self, loss or reduction of gratification in previously gratifying activities, loss of emotional attachment, and often crying spells. Cognitive manifestations refer to a person's distorted attitudes toward him/herself, his/her experience, and his/her future, a person's self-blaming notion of causality, and difficulties in decision making. Cognitive manifestations include low self-evaluation, negative expectations, self-blame and self-criticism, indecisiveness, and a distorted view of body image. Still a powerful aspect of depression, and one that is of extreme importance to young African-American males, is the motivational manifestations. Motivational manifestations include strivings, desires, and impulses that are consciously experienced. A key feature of the quality of motivation of the depressed person is its regressive nature. Depression tends to draw him/her to activities that are the least demanding in terms of degree of responsibility or initiative required, or the amount of energy to be expended. The motivationally depressed person seeks to escape from problems rather than trying to solve them, and seeks immediate, but transient, gratification instead of delayed, but prolonged, gratification. Motivational manifestations include paralysis of will, avoidance, escapist and withdrawal wishes, suicidal wishes, and increased dependency.

Beck (1976) offers a useful framework for viewing the connections between the cognitive aspects of depression and the associated affective, motivational, and physical phenomena of depression. I find this framework especially useful for viewing the experience of depression as it relates to Black young men. Beck outlines three major cognitive patterns that force the individual to view himself, his world, and his future idiosyncratically. This triad of patterns *The Primary Triad* consists of, (1) the pattern of construing experiences in a negative way, (2) the pattern of viewing himself in a negative way, and (3) the pattern of viewing his future in a negative way. All three aspects of this paradigm are relative or applicable to young Black men, who endure the resulting depressive states often into adulthood without ever having appropriate psychiatric attention.

ANGER

Webster's Dictionary offers a brief definition of anger: "a strong passion or emotion excited by injury." Averill (1982) offers a more concise definition of anger: "Anger may be defined as a conflictive emotion that on the biological level, is related to aggressive systems and, even more important, to the capacities for cooperative social living, symbolization, and reflective self-awareness; that, on the psychological level, is aimed at the correction of some appraised wrong; and that, on the sociocultural level, functions to uphold accepted standards of conduct" (p. 317). It is clear that this definition speaks to the subjective experience of anger while respecting its physiological aspects. *The Dictionary of Concepts in General Psychology* (1988) states that anger consists of two components: disquieting subjective feelings and an awareness of physiological reactions that is characteristic of all emotion.

Anger can be expressed in a variety of ways. Physical attacks and violence, verbal abuse, withdrawal, manipulation, denying someone a benefit or something desired, raising one's voice, telling a third party, and discussing a conflict are all examples of how anger can be expressed. Anger can also find expression through dance. Anger has historically been defined as either the subjective experience that accompanies aggression, as a state of physiological arousal that enhances the probability of aggression, or as an intervening variable that mediates the effects of frustration. In the Yale frustration-aggression hypothesis study (1939) very little attention is given to anger. It is referenced in the index only once and that reference was to a footnote that does not mention anger specifically. Anger therefore, was not a relevant consideration in the Yale study on Frustration and Aggression (Averill, 1982; Dollard et al., 1939). Berkowitz (1962), in his reformulation of the frustration-aggression hypothesis, reintroduced the concept of anger as an intermediary of frustration and aggression. According to Averill (1982), this introduction of anger, as a "drive which heightens the likelihood of aggressive behavior" (p. 128), serves to strip anger of most of its meaning. In other words, according to this conception, frustration creates a predisposition to make hostile responses by arousing anger (a heightened state of physiological arousal), which, in the presence of appropriate environmental stimuli, may lead to aggression. To Averill, this is an over interpretation of the fact that frustration is one of the factors most frequently cited as being involved in instigating anger. A biological perspective, although valid, may not be the complete story in that society plays a significant role in shaping the individual. To the extent that anger is a socially constituted syndrome, a thorough discussion of anger from a biological perspective would have to take into consideration the evolution of human cognitive capacities, symbolization, and cooperative social living, as well as the evolution of aggression (Averill, 1982; Baggio, 1987).

Theories on anger fall into general categories of five theories on the nature of emotional response. They are the (1) physiological traditional theories (Ax, 1953; Durel & Krantz, 1985; James, 1893, 1894; Wolf, 1973), which include those that define emotion consistently and exclusively in physiological terms, (2) facial feedback theories (Eckman, Friesen, & Ellsworth, 1972; Laird, 1974; Leventhal, 1980), which hold that facial feedback is actually our awareness of the subjective experience of a specific emotion, (3) two factor (cognition-plus arousal) theory (Novaco, 1979; Russell, 1961; Schachter, 1964) which holds that given a state of physiological arousal for which an individual has no immediate explanation, he will label this state and describe his feelings in terms of the cognitions available to him, (4) psycho-

analytic theory (Kellerman, 1979; Storr, 1968) which deals with the relationship between intrapsychic process and discharge of psychic tension otherwise seen as affect, and (5) subjectivist theories (Buck, 1980; Buck, 1983;
Hohmann, 1966) which look at emotion as a function of subjective experience.

Emotions can be defined as socially constituted syndromes which include
an individual's appraisal of the situation and which are interpreted as pas-
sions, rather than as actions (Averill, 1980). Leventhal (1980, 1983) also
focuses on perceptual indicators while defining emotions as subjective perceptual experiences that are mediated by motor processes, memories of previous emotional experiences, and conceptual processes. Leventhal's perceptual-motor theory of emotion was a useful tool in conceptualizing and providing a basis for addressing treatment considerations for anger within the
context of the author's study.

In the perceptual-motor theory there are three mechanisms or processes
that are thought to interact simultaneously in contributing to the experience
of emotion (Baggio, 1987). Initially, there is the expressive-motor processing
system, which is the primary generator of subjective feeling. In this system,
expressive motor reactions serve as a source of affective experience for the
individual. Secondly, there is the mechanism of schematic processing, which
is responsible for processing perceptual-motor memories of actual emotional
experiences. This can be seen as a record of conditioned emotional reactions,
which include stimulus representations, subjective feelings, and motor reactions that are conditioned classically. From a neurological viewpoint, the
conditioned emotional and motor reactivity can be understood in the concept
of neuroplasticity which can include negative neuroplasticity. Through this
process, the repertory of situational events capable of eliciting emotional
reactions is accumulated. The third mechanism is conceptual processing,
which is a repository of memories and operations about feelings, and is
responsible for production of attitudes or evaluations from specific emotional
experiences.

This conceptualization of anger views anger as a subjective perceptual
experience that can be modified by a number of strategies. There are two
major strategies for regulation and control of the expressive-motor, schematic, and autonomic levels of emotional functioning (Leventhal & Mosbach,
1983): (1) regulation of stimulation; and (2) regulation of motor responses.
Bohart (1980) offers a clinical view of this perspective in that there are two
means by which an individual can remove the sense of perceived threat that
accompanies anger; by (1) coping with either the threat-inducing situation or
person, or by (2) changing one's attitude or understanding of the situation. In
treating anger it is important to be specific as to the goal, considering the fact
that level of anger arousal can be both normative and maladaptive. Some
individuals respond angrily at higher frequencies, greater intensity, and long-

er duration than others and have a response style that can have a highly disruptive effect on their mental and physical health as well as on their capacity to cope effectively with the stimulus producing situation. While some individuals respond angrily without reasonable justification, others do respond reasonably and adaptively to particular provocation. The clinician must evaluate whether or not the given response is justifiable or unjustifiable. This requires an understanding of the context in which the provocation occurred and an evaluation of the appropriateness of the individual's response to it. Many Black youth are faced with situations where even if the response is a justifiable one, it may still contribute to a harmful outcome, or even to their death.

There are clearly situations (rape, theft, etc.) which justify anger. However, there are situations that are not always so clear. An individual may respond angrily to a fairly innocuous stimulus. In this instance it is up to the clinician to discern whether the stimulus has some cue value to the individual, because what may seem, at a surface level, to be an unjustified response may actually be a reasonable one, considering the context and the individual's history. If the anger response is justified it becomes important for the clinician to assist the individual in finding a constructive means of coping with the provocation.

I recall Dr. DeGruy-Leary's telling a story (in her book, *Post Traumatic Slave Syndrome*) about a theatre incident as an illustration of the "ever present anger" many African Americans experience. The incident involved a group of friends sitting in a row between two groups of white teens who were throwing popcorn at each other. She was hit in the face with a piece of popcorn which prompted one of the young men with them to turn around with "menace" in his eyes. His entire body language and facial expression had changed. As he began to rise from his seat she gently touched his arm, stopping him and said "It was only popcorn." Had she not acted, this young man would probably have verbally or physically assaulted someone.

DeGruy-Leary goes on to discuss the idea that no matter what we are doing the anger is rarely far away. "Its as if there is a wellspring of anger that lies just below the surface of many African Americans and it doesn't take much for it to emerge and be expressed. This seems to be especially true for many Black men."

I clearly understood the young man... and at a point in my life would have responded to the popcorn incident similarly, with the exception that I might not have been so easily stopped. Although I'm not sure how historically astute the young man in question was, I'm sure that given the knowledge I held in my early twenties, of the indignities and atrocities suffered by Black women during our sojourn in America, an older Black woman in my company being disrespected (hit by popcorn) by a group of white youngsters would've been a trigger for a level of anger already at threshold.

The history of assaults as well as the current day assaults serve to maintain the anger at threshold. This is seen in the many Black men I've come in contact with who are caught up in one legal system or another. The family court system serves as a typical anger provoking trap for all too many Black men. Some have described the institution as a "roach motel"; easy to get in and very difficult to get out! Many Black men who are solid fathers and who, for whatever reason, live separate and apart from their child's mother are brought through the court system at the discretion of the child's mother. Once this occurs, all fathers are painted with the broad brush of "dead beat dad" and treated as such. Many find their bank accounts levied, face garnishment of their paychecks and are threatened with revocation of their driver's license; impacting their means of transportation while facing the need to maintain their employment or find work. Dealing with anger becomes a therapeutic issue for Black Americans whether in the context of family relationships, the couples dynamic, as an individual or the relationship with this country's institutions.

Although anger has been looked upon, in general, as a negative emotion, it can serve some extremely important adaptive functions. Novaco (1976) has noted some beneficial effects of anger that are of particular importance to young African-American males. They are as follows: (1) the energizing effect of anger can enable a person to assertively confront provocation or injustice; (2) demonstrations of anger advertise potency, expressiveness, and determination; (3) anxious feelings of vulnerability are preempted by the arousal of anger; and (4) anger can potentiate a sense of personal control.

Anger, however, is often suppressed by African-Americans in general, and by young African-American males in particular. That is, given a provocation to which an angry response would generally be justified, these individuals suppress the experience and the expression of anger. This suppression may have extremely negative psychological consequences for the individual, such as a sense of powerlessness or loss of self-esteem, as well as physical and relational consequences, such as disturbed interpersonal relationships, passive-aggressive response patterns, psychosomatic and other health related symptoms (Baggio, 1987; Averill, 1982).

As the above discussion clearly indicates, the experience of anger is a complicated clinical issue and, at the same time, a challenging one. It is an obstacle we must tackle, however, if we are to effectively work with and impact the lives of young African-American males.

Chapter Six

Violence Prevention: Historical Context of Violence Prevention

Although violence in the United States of America is historical, the field of violence prevention is relatively new. Violence prevention seems to be an outgrowth of general interventions designed to improve social competence, which include basic social skills training programs and approaches that focus specifically on the prevention of aggression (Hammond & Yung, 1993). Many of these skill-based programs, however, were developed and designed for and are targeted to White middle-class populations. Despite three decades of existence, they have been mostly ineffective at reducing health damaging behaviors (Mills, Dunham, & Alpert, 1988; Rhodes & Jason, 1988). For African-American youth, relevant violence prevention programming that address their particular issues has been quite limited.

There have been several barriers to the development of violence prevention methodologies for African-American youth. One of the most fundamental barriers has been the way in which violence is traditionally defined and viewed. Traditional attempts to separate American society from the violence it produces has created barriers to viewing its prevention as an appropriate issue for the health care system. The "blame the victim" approach encompasses a belief and assumptions that criminals, or perpetrators of violence, are deviants who engage in such activities in service to their own self-centered ends and are determined to disrupt the peaceful and orderly functioning of society. This view, that criminal and violent activity is initiated and sustained by a "distinct outlaw class of criminal personalities who are at war against an innocent and decent" society of normal persons, has spawned such "overworked" and ineffective approaches as "just say no to drugs," "war on poverty," and "war on drugs" (Wilson, 1990). War is very much a Western European ethos. But when it comes to tragedies like the mass murders at

Sandy Hook Elementary school, who do we, as a society, make war against? On the morning of December 14, 2012, a young man (Adam Lanza), after shooting and killing his mother, entered the grounds of Sandy Hook Elementary School in the small town of Newtown, Connecticut. He was heavily armed and by the time he had completed his shooting rampage, twenty children and six adults would lose their lives. He then turned the gun on himself committing suicide. Lanza, who lived with his mother, had been diagnosed with Asperger's syndrome and had grown more and more reclusive. What is known of his life reveals (more-than-likely) deeper psychological issues. An investigation of Lanza indicated that he had pursued increasingly odd and violent interests. His computer revealed fascination with the military and weapons, with mass murders, with a school shooting video game and with other odd perverse media. He had posted numerous times on a website dedicated to mass killings revealing a completely deranged worldview. Only months prior to the Sandy Hook shooting incident, twelve moviegoers were killed seeing a Batman movie in Colorado and six people were killed attending a Sikh temple in Wisconsin. None of these shooters were Black men. As a matter of fact, with the exception of the recent shooting in September 2013 at the naval yard in Washington, very few shooters have been Black men. Yet stereotypes continue to drive approaches to violence prevention that fails to consider issues of mental health and access to weapons and ammunition with the capacity for mass killings. Instead, discussions focused on increased weaponization of school environments are treated in the public discourse as credible. Theories that inform program development, which view violence as an outcome of a deviant community or that blame the victim, have failed to address pertinent issues of violence and have been largely ineffective in creating relevant programs (Issacs, 1992). Quite to the contrary, these ideas have fueled the *School to Prison* pipeline. It is telling that 40% of students expelled from schools in the U.S. are Black; that 70% of students involved in "in-school" arrests or who are referred to law enforcement while in school are Black or Latino; that Black students are three-and-one-half times more likely to be suspended than White students and that Black and Latino youth are twice as likely to not graduate high school than White students (NAACP-LDF, 2012; ACLU, 2008; PBS, 2013). Similar statistics exists for youth who move from foster care to prison (PBS, 2013).

The lack of an advocacy base has also been a barrier to a national preventive focus (Spivak et al., 1989). One reason for this may be because victims of homicide and intentional injury are largely people living in poverty. People living in poverty tend to be preoccupied with surviving, which often precludes social and political organizing. Nor does this group have the economic wherewithal to form well-financed political action committees or to finance legislation. The parents and advocates of the victims of the Sandy Hook shooting had an extremely high profile and along with congresswoman

Gabriel "Gabby" Gifford and her husband, pushed for meetings with congress. The tragedy commanded an unusual degree of media attention. Indeed, advocates for sensible gun laws even had the ear of the President. Yet, as of this writing, they have been unable to have an impact of any significance on gun legislation given the power and wealth of the gun industry and its influence in congress. America has handled the issue of violence much like the issue of substance abuse, in that its systems have a tendency to not respond until the crisis hits middle class America. And even then, policy change is a heavy lift. Those in poverty have even less of a chance of enacting substantive change at the level of national policy.

Still, a very important barrier to the development of violence prevention methodology for African-American youth has been the need to re-educate the public health and mental health professionals, teachers, and others involved with African-American youth, in a way that will give them a better understanding of violence and the tools necessary to resolve issues of conflict and violence. Because violence has been viewed primarily from a criminal justice perspective it becomes easy for those who lack the skills and proper framework to effectively deal with violent behavior to defer to the criminal justice system.

RESEARCH IN VIOLENCE PREVENTION

Research in the area of violence prevention is relatively new, but attempts to predict male delinquent and violent behavior date as far back as the 1950's (Glueck & Glueck, 1950; Hakeem, 1957, 1958; Loeber & Dishion, 1983). Some early researchers believed that the use of psychometrics could be invaluable in the prediction of violent behavior, but such substantial claims have been criticized on methodological grounds (Hirschi & Selvin, 1967).

Prediction research in violence and delinquency has occurred largely in the arena of criminology. Its primary focus has been on identifying behaviors that are continuous over time. Monahan (1989) divides the most current body of research in prediction of violent behavior into *first and second-generation* research studies. This *first generation* of studies which were conducted in the 1970's, although highly flawed in terms of predictive accuracy, were part of a national shift from a focus on need for treatment to prediction of dangerousness. Monahan writes:

> A decade ago a national movement was afoot to revise the criteria for civil commitment away from an assessment of a "need for treatment" and toward a prediction of "dangerousness" to others or to self. So appealing to the legal mind was the libertarian logic of the dangerousness model that by the mid-1970's virtually every state had, if not entirely thrown over need for treatment

in favor of dangerousness, at least grafted dangerousness on to its existing standards for commitment. (p. 10)

Second generation thinking on prediction is considerably more reserved in its claims of accuracy but focuses on the possibility of predicting accurately enough to be useful in some policy decisions.

Loeber and Dishion (1983) rank ordered predictors of delinquency and listed them as (1) composite measures of parental family management techniques; (2) child problem behavior; (3) stealing, lying, or truancy; (4) criminality or anti-social behavior of family members; (5) poor educational achievement; (6) single measures of parental family management; (7) separation from parents; and (8) socioeconomic status.

What is important about research in the prediction of violent/delinquent behavior is how it is used. If it is used merely for attempts at identification of those members of society who may be prone to violence, we must ethically ask the question, what will be done with them once they are identified? Will society isolate them based on the probability of future anti-social or violent behavior as it does those who actually become violent or anti-social? Or will society go further and begin to address the root causes of such predictors, thereby setting policy for prevention of violent behavior? Given the well documented history of racism in the field of psychology, the misuse of psychometric tools, and of racist scientific theories (Guthrie, 1976; Hilliard, 1991; Nobles, 1991), it is extremely important that the purpose of predictive research be clear, well defined, and resistant to following the path of predecessors that have historically conducted an assault on African people.

Despite Darwin's belief that there were no defined differences between species, let alone races, polygenetic theorists exploited the new evolutionary zeitgeist shaping evolution as a new thinking that would grow to become known as "scientific racism." Carried forward in the nineteenth and twentieth centuries by well-known scientists and pseudo-scientists the likes of Francis Galton, "scientific racism" laid the groundwork for a bevy of "race" related theories claiming racial superiority for Teutonic or Nordic (Aryan) peoples. Racist thinkers like Gobineau (1816-1882) and later, Chamberlain (1855-1927) extended the promotion of Aryan superiority (Jackson Jr. and Weidman, 2006). Notions of pure heredity separate and apart from environmental influences and of Nordic supremacy would fuel the eugenicist movement especially in the United States and Germany. Members of the eugenicist movement included very prominent and aristocratic citizens, some who, like Darwin and Madison Grant, were not trained scientists but wealthy enough to dabble in their areas of interest. Nevertheless they had a profound impact on enacting racist policies on immigration and sterilization. Those of lower socioeconomic status did not fare well under eugenic policies regardless of race. However, it is the interweaving of pseudo-scientific eugenicist ideas of racial inferiority with ideas around inherent black criminality that serve as a basis for how Black people came to be viewed as a criminal class despite the statistical reality and history of white crime (Mohammad, 2013). The fact that African Americans are overrepresented in the ranks of lower socioeconomic status and the undereducated in America makes this issue all the more salient. Especially when such positioning has been by design.

Factors that predict or contribute to violence can be explored in the service of developing and initiating prevention approaches. To motivate this, violence must be reconceptualized and seen as a public health issue, recognizing the role of oppression, discrimination, poverty, adverse societal norms, as well as psychiatric syndromes in its development and perpetuation. A useful conceptual framework in the service of violence prevention would be a public health model. Spivak et al (1989) discuss the public health model as one that presents violence as a learned response to the environmental sources of stress. Hammond and Yung (1993) take the explanation a step further in describing the public health model as one that recognizes host, agent, and environment as elements of a health problem that are interdependent. These three elements, when combined in a public health framework, recognize the reciprocity between the individual and environment with respect to the individual's effect on his or her environment and the environment's influence on the development and maintenance of certain behavior.

Issues, which relate to the environment, have to do with socio-cultural and economic factors within the environment that contribute to assaultive violence among young African-American males. Factors closely associated with poverty such as community disorganization, joblessness, family dysfunction, and high population density are indicated in accounting for high rates of violence within urban settings (Messner & Sampson, 1991). The exact role of ethnicity as a predictor for assaultive violence is unclear. There is also debate as to the presence or absence of racial-ethnic differences once socioeconomic status is controlled. However, there is no debate about the violent environment Black/African people have had to endure and survive throughout the diaspora starting with chattel slavery up to the modern day. Socioeconomically, it is clear that young African-American males remain at excessive risk in that they are overrepresented in the population of families living below the poverty level (Hammond & Yung, 1993).

The agent element has to do with the physical mechanism or object used to commit the act of assault. In the United States, the agent or weapon most widely used is a gun (Hammond & Yung, 1993). Unfortunately, all too often, the weapons of choice are automatic rifles and pistols capable of massive damage before reloading.

A significant set of factors relate to the host. These elements associated with violence lie in the psychosocial and/or biological realm. They contribute to young African-American males' level of risk for becoming victims or perpetrators of assaultive violence. Research on cognitive processes related to assaultive violence indicates, among other variables, those having to do with the individual's perception. Graham and Hudley's (1992) study on attributes to aggression found that African-American young men who were identified as aggressive by their peers showed a greater likelihood for believing that a peer member's intent was malicious. In addition, they endorsed aggressive responses to perceived provocation. For many Black young men, respect is a very important and sensitive issue in that they have been effectively cut off from socially sanctioned means of gaining community respect. Much has been written on the myriad of methods used to emasculate the Black man including the assault and brutal rape of the Black woman in his presence. All too often, his choice was to act and die with the possibility of several others being killed as an example or to live another day traumatized. The Black woman faced a whole other set of traumatic variables including her death and the possible death of her children if she resisted. For the slave and his ancestry many years after the official end of slavery, life was a constant, day-to-day experience of degradation and deprivation in the service of white power and the ideal of white supremacy. What little respect a man could muster in his environment had to be clung too. Along with unhealthy models of aggression and brutality exhibited by stewards of the slave system, the critical need to salvage a fractured sense of respect has resulted in unhealthy and destructive behavioral patterns associated with the maintenance of respect/fear.

Unfortunately, many young Black men perceive most places as environments capable of engendering violent experiences. Similarly, May's (1986) study on cognitive processes and violent behavior in adolescent males found that perceptual bias (a psychological disposition related to the tendency to perceive violence), rather than response bias, was a possible maintaining factor in the presentation of aggressive and violent behavior. All too often, behavioral slights or mistakes are taken as acts of aggression. How many times have we heard of a youth being shot to death because he stepped on another's tennis shoes or may have bumped someone while walking. This was certainly the tragic case that ended the life of Chicago basketball star Ben Wilson in 1984. I remember living in Chicago at the time the young Wilson was named top high school basketball player in the country. I also remember how this seemingly senseless tragedy touched many in the city, as over 10,000 mourners would show up at the 6'8" basketball star's services. Many more called to an end to gang violence.

Another cognitive factor found to mediate aggression has been the individual's likelihood to believe aggression increases self-esteem. In addition to individual perception, anger and rejection have been indicated as being associated with violent aggressive behavior, and in association with the experience of poverty and racism, anger can also lower the individual's threshold for violence (Akbar, 1980; Slaby & Guerra, 1988).

The variables cited above, along with dysthymic and depressed moods, have been found to affect the patterns of thinking and styles of interaction that support verbal and/or physical conflict. Hammond and Yung (1993), among others, make the case for the development of interventions that address these factors versus the long-term adverse consequences that may occur in the absence of such interventions.

Programs that Indicate Positive Outcome

There are successful precedents for such a proposed program. The Hawk Federation, a rites of passage program sponsored by the Institute for the Advanced Study of Black Family Life and Culture, Inc., holds that it is important to provide the developmental experience(s) that are necessary for the proper physical and intellectual growth and development of the young Black male. The Institute believes that successful prevention activities must alter the negative images, ideas, and values that are imposed upon Black males and develop strategies designed to break the cycle of apathy, despair, and hopelessness that pervades many of the urban communities and place the Black male at risk. The Institute supports the premise that the foundation of all behavior is a set of *ideas*, which give the behavior license and direction. The Hawk program offered inner-city youth a structured program and environment where their attitudes and beliefs are impacted by the introduction of culturally relevant information, culturally sensitive process, and the utilization of mentors and models who emulate Afrocentric principles. The Hawk program's use of culturally relevant information and culturally sensitive process was similar to the usage in and helped serve as a model for the author's study. A slight difference is that the author considered the average adolescent's high level of exposure to media in developing and structuring the intervention. The Hawk program has proven successful within the educational arena documenting increase in GPA and by improved teacher reports (Nobles, 1989).

A consideration and utilization of protective factors that are culturally relevant is indicated in the development of treatment methodology (Issacs, 1992). Some early protective factors observed by researchers include the following: (1) early primary relationships that promote social development, (2) experiences that promote affective development, (3) promotion of cultural awareness and positive cultural identity, and (4) an explicit value system that influences the avoidance of violence. Instilling an Afrocentric value system can be instrumental in promoting a positive cultural identity and a sense of self-protection in young people, which can have an impact on future involvement in violence. The Hawk Federation Project utilizes such a value system. The Hawk project was developed to address problems experienced in the Black community while reflecting its historical and cultural integrity. Nobles (1989), writes:

> It is the opinion of the Institute that social deviancy, pathology, substance abuse, inappropriate behavior, sexual misconduct, hopelessness, defeatism, etc. are all exacerbated by racism and exploitation and like racist behavior, they are all grounded in the American culture. Hence, the task of changing the inappropriate behavior is, in effect, a task of 'culturally realigning' (reconnecting one with one's spiritual base in that African philosophy holds that there is a spiritual essence which underlies, and incorporates all material phenomena) the adolescent's behavior with principles of conduct consistent with the highest level of human functioning. In effect, aberrant behavior, which is based on culturally distorted ideas, must be realigned with culturally accurate and appropriate 'ideas.' The development of the HAWK Federation is consistent with this strategy. (p. 8)

In the Hawk project the young males are introduced to the cardinal virtues of MAAT, which is the framework of interconnecting principles about the nature of humans, the earth, and the universe, which the ancient Africans developed and lived by. There are several conceptual and practical pillars in the structure of Maatian ethics which include: (1) the concept and practice of Maat itself, (2) the early and evolved concept and practice of righteous leadership rooted in service, (3) philosophical anthropology and the essentiality of learning and practice, and (4) the seven cardinal virtues which sustain Maatian practice. The seven cardinal virtues are truth, justice, righteousness, propriety, balance, harmony or reciprocity, and order (Karenga, 1990; Nobles, 1989).

These are the types of principles that can, and do, promote changes in the attitudes, beliefs, and subsequent behaviors of young African-American males. These principles can be utilized in the prevention of deviant, violent behavior. Like the principles introduced in the proposed program and study, they are embedded in an Afrocentric methodological framework. Moreover, these Afrocentric principles as represented in the Hawk Project and in the proposed program are targeted toward healing the spirit or the Sakhu (Nobles, 2013).

The Progressive Life Center (founded in 1983 and based in Washington, DC) utilizes creative and successful strategies in the treatment of mental health related problems within the Black community. The Progressive Life Foundation incorporates the Bantu concept of *NTU*, which stands for essence. It exemplifies the fundamental African philosophy that there is a spiritual essence, which underlies, and incorporates, all material phenomena. Progressive Life Foundation, under the direction of Dr. Fred Phillips, uses NTU to highlight the interrelatedness between the intrinsic and extrinsic factors that impact one's ability to influence and respond to problems of daily living. Progressive Life Foundation developed NTU as its philosophical framework for delivering spiritually based, culturally centered and family-centered psychological services. NTU Psychotherapy is based on core principles of ancient African worldview, nurtured through African-American culture, and augmented by Western conceptualizations of Humanistic psychology. These core principles of mental health and healing are: Harmony, Balance, Interconnectedness, and Authenticity. These principles, along with the Nguzo Saba (Seven Principles) developed by Maulana R. Karenga out of the same tradition, are utilized to introduce adolescents to culturally based traditions, rituals, and practices. The result is a deepening of their connection to their cultural history, identity, and their individual potential. Progressive Life offers a host of professional services including psychotherapy, counseling, assessment, training, and therapeutic foster care meeting the clinical, mental health and human service needs of youth and families regardless of ethnicity. In addition, special programs are offered which include therapeutic retreats, rites of passage, parent training, NTU training, family preservation, and AIDS related services. The rites of passage program introduces adolescents to culturally based traditions, rituals, and practices, which deepen their connection to their cultural history, identity, and individual potential. Male and female participants improve self-esteem, communication, and problem-solving skills through their involvement in an intensive and active Afrocentric learning experience. These programs represent interventions designed to alter the patterns of thought and styles of interaction that tend to support verbal or physical conflict. Underlying these interventions are the universal principles, spiritual focus and cultural awareness of NTU. This can be witnessed in the success of such programs as the NIA Foster Care Program and the Family Preservation Program (PLC, 2009).

One example of a program aimed at impacting interactions associated with violence is the Violence Prevention Project of the Health Promotion Program for Urban Youth in Boston. This program is directed at reducing the incidence of violent behavior and associated social and medical hazards for adolescents. It is a community-based primary prevention effort directed at changing individual behavior and community attitudes around violence through outreach and education. The violence prevention curriculum is specifically aimed at raising the individual threshold for violence by creating a nonviolent ethos within the classroom and by expanding the repertoire of responses to anger. Students are not taught to become passive agents, but rather are expected to claim their anger and become intentional and creative in their response to it.

Perhaps such programs have been appropriate for impacting behavioral change and/or academic performance, but what of the intra-psychic processes that are certainly the concern of the field of psychology? Could it be that there are aspects of such programs that do hold significant treatment possibilities for mental health practitioners; especially those whose major work is with the population referred to as the "lost generation," (Black adolescents and young adults)? The author's study contains methodology that could have tremendous impact on the development and expansion of treatment possibilities for this population in particular and other ethnic minority youth populations in general. This is especially the case among Latino/Native American youth who have had to survive and respond to European hegemony and the ongoing legacy of white supremacy. Youth, who lack the intra-psychic resilience necessary to tolerate frustration, appropriately manage their anger, and deal with depression could certainly benefit from the development of such methodologies.

The fields of psychological and sociological study provide a wide body of literature indicating frustration, anger, and depression as important factors in the presentation of violent behavior, lowered self-esteem, and destructive behavior. Research focusing on the areas of frustration tolerance, anger mediation, and depression can have tremendous implications for the development of cognitive techniques. Further, the development of culturally relevant methodology for the treatment of depression, the constructive mediation of anger, and the development of frustration tolerance, could have tremendous impact for the treatment of young Black males, including those who are institutionalized. Such treatment designs may also impact the planning and development of violence prevention strategies. In any case, given the scale of the crisis, it is well worth the effort.

Chapter Seven

Standard Approaches, Implications for Violence Intervention and the Need for Cultural Relevance

Black-on-Black teen homicide is at an all-time high. Still, very little has been done within the criminal justice and legislative fields to assist young Black males in handling environmental cues differently. Strategies have been limited to the threat of punishment and law enforcement as a perceived deterrent. Rehabilitation has been secondary as an intervention measure and has not had sufficient focus on cognitive processes associated with violent behavior.

When we look at the fact that drugs, youth gangs, violence, victimization, and crime are increasingly becoming part of the everyday experiences of Black males, it becomes incumbent on researchers and experts in the field of prevention and intervention to take a closer look at what has and has not worked, what are the causes of such violence, and what may be promising approaches to decreasing and eventually eradicating violence among this population.

Nationally, programs that aim at juvenile delinquency and violence prevention have shown little evidence of long-term effectiveness (Zigler, Taussig, & Black, 1992). Many of these programs had been developed as an outgrowth of punitive "tough on crime" policies, which do not appear to have made an impact. This was especially true of California, which ranked among the most punitive and neglectful of states in the way it treated its high-risk youth, boasting 20% of all juveniles incarcerated in the entire nation (Petersilia, 1992) some twenty years ago. In 2006, a team of nationally recognized experts put together to help implement court-ordered reforms in California observed "This is a system that is broken almost everywhere you look," listing eighteen severe and systemic deficiencies (Mendel, 2011). Parole violations played a role in increased incarceration rates also. By 2006 California had both the largest absolute number and percentage increase of admissions for parole violations. The number of inmates swelled to the point where in 2011 the Supreme Court ordered the California Department of Corrections to take actions to reduce its state prison overcrowding to at least 137% capacity. As a result of this and other national movement towards intervention versus sentencing for non-violent offenders we have seen an overall drop in youth incarceration. Although the United States still leads the industrialized world in the rate at which we lock up our young and Black youth are still five times more likely to be locked up than their white counterparts, in 2010 the rate of youth confinement reached a thirty-five-year low (Casey Foundation, 2013; Shelden & Teji, 2012; CDCR; 2010). Contrary to popular assumptions about more incarceration resulting in less crime, California's juvenile crime rate has substantially declined during its period of rapid de-incarceration from 1999-2008.

This tough on crime approach has dominated national crime policy since the late 1970s, steering the national focus and valuable resources away from addressing the root causes of crime and the rehabilitation of criminals. In reality, the justice system has played a relatively limited role in crime control. Overall the recidivism evidence clearly indicates that confinement in youth corrections facilities doesn't work as a strategy for keeping youth away from crime. Its punitive treatment of juveniles, especially Black youth, has been entirely inconsistent with the growing body of evidence related to the causes of juvenile delinquency and violence (Greenwood, 1992, Mendel, 2011).

Factors such as frustration tolerance, depression, and anger have implications for degree of uncooperativeness, school performance, aggression, passive-aggressive behavior, and disturbed interpersonal relationships; all ingredients that can land a youth into a correctional facility. However, very little research has been done on culturally sensitive interventions aimed at reducing these factors in Black adolescent males (Baggio, 1987; Davies, 1989, Muran, Kassinove, Ross, & Muran, 1989).

Interventions that focus on the reduction of risk factors such as high unemployment, poverty, or poor housing are normally evaluated along outcome measures such as decrease in reported homicides or violent incidents. However, exploration of cognitive mechanisms associated with violent/delinquent behavior is not a normal component of the evaluation process of such programs. Since attitudes, perceptions, and beliefs are indicated in the mediation of outcome response to environmental cues (Ellis, 1962; Nobles 1987), it seems reasonable that interventions designed to ultimately reduce violent and delinquent behavior would impact these variables. As a result of seeking to impact violent behavior by addressing the behavior to the exclusion of the associated frustration, depression, and delinquency, violence prevention methodologies have not been very successful.

However, when it comes to recidivism, researchers have found certain program characteristics that tend to be effective. Findings indicate that programs offering counseling and treatment tend to reduce recidivism while programs focused on coercion and control tended to produce weak, negative or no results. Programs that address specific risk factors, like the ones listed above, tend to succeed. Programs that offer cognitive behavioral therapies (CBT) tend to produce a significant reduction in recidivism. Evidence-based models like Multi-systemic Therapy, Functional Family Therapy and Multi-dimensional Treatment Foster Care have also shown promise in reduction of recidivism (Mendel, 2011).

In light of the current epidemic of violence among Black youth, we must take a closer look at approaches that have shown promise and work to develop creative, culturally relevant, and efficient programs that speak to the needs of young Black males and that address some of the causes of violence.

Many authors have expressed the need for the field of mental health to play a contributory role in response to violence (Farrington, 1986; Fitzpatrick & Boldizar, 1993; Hammond & Yung, 1993; Isaac, 1992; May 1986; Spivak et al., 1989). There is great need for psychology to face the challenge of designing, implementing, and evaluating programs and techniques aimed at influencing non-violent behavior. If the task of the mental health system is to facilitate the individual's return to a state of mental/emotional health and balance (Braxton, 1992), then there are two options for managing the state of imbalance and disorder. The mental health system can attempt to control the situation externally, colluding with the criminal justice system. In doing so, it will characterize and label violent offenders as deviant personalities, which, like a cancer, must be cut off from a society of "normal," "peace-loving" people. On the other hand, the mental health system can assist the individual, putting some level of order into his/her internal world, thereby having the individual eventually regain control of his/her life.

Reggie was an African American young man in his second year of high school.[1] He was court referred to our community clinic due to truancy behavior and fighting behavior. A mental health technician working for the juvenile court had evaluated Reggie. She had diagnosed the young man as bipolar and added that he also expressed anti-social tendencies. Much of this opinion was predicated on the clinical interview where Reggie was asked about his rap music (he had been practicing and writing and considered himself a rapper).

As I interviewed Reggie it became apparent that he was a bright and passionate young man. It had also become apparent that the psychiatric services provider contracted by the court had grossly misread this case. Reggie was a young teenager in a great deal of pain who had been experiencing much of the criteria for Post-Traumatic Stress Disorder (PTSD) for quite some time. Mostly due to his moodiness, his tendency to fight and a misperception of the appropriateness of his affect, he had been incorrectly labeled. When interviewed by the court's mental health assessor, Reggie used terms like "I'm sick with this! I come sick with this shit! I got stupid dope rhymes. I'm-a kill it!" when referring to his lyrics and rap style. Because of his manner of expression he had been identified as having morbid content.

Upon closer review, Reggie was a young man with a tragic past, who had been carrying a great deal of guilt, pain, loss and anger with him. When Reggie was about five years of age, he had gone with his mother to an apartment building. He waited outside on the lawn while his mother went up the stairs (which were visible from the outside of the building) to the second floor. He witnessed an altercation between his mother and at least two other people. He then witnessed his mother being pushed as she fell down the stairs to her death. He expressed feeling powerless to intervene. He also remembered going to court but came to realize that the people responsible for his mother's murder were never found guilty and jailed.

Reggie expressed that he had trouble sleeping over the years and that he would experience unwanted, intrusive thoughts often throughout the day. These thoughts negatively impacted his ability to focus in school and he appeared physically tired during our early sessions. His relationship with his father was strained as he maintained a level of anger at his father's perceived failure to protect and avenge his mother's death. He also dealt with significant self-blame as he experienced trouble shaking the belief that he should have been able to do something to change the course of events.

Creating rap lyrics was not only his means of expression but it was his way of displacing unwanted thoughts and recurring images of his mother's death. Reggie was a good example of a child who was never a menace, but someone who was crying out for help, if only we in mental health possessed the cultural sensitivity to hear him.

There is an increasing call for cultural sensitivity in prevention and treatment services for ethnic minorities. Although the relative number of violence prevention programs designed specifically for young African-American men are few, they have shown some evidence of success in decreasing violent/aggressive behavior (Hammond & Yung, 1993; Wilson-Brewer, 1992). Wilson-Brewer (1992) in her chapter on prevention programs in *The Impact of Community Violence on African American Children and Families*, outlines four basic categories of intervention strategies for violence prevention: educational interventions, recreational interventions, environmental/technical interventions, and legal interventions. Educational interventions include some of the newest and most common approaches to violence prevention and tend to be the approaches that incorporate Afrocentric emphasis. They include mentoring programs, rites of passage programs, manhood training programs, conflict resolution, mediation education, and public awareness education programs. Some of these programs operate on methodology impacting psychological structures. For this reason, I would expand the nomenclature for this category, preferring to use the term *psycho-educational* interventions. However, programs with an Afrocentric emphasis have been subject to some of the same criticisms as other violence prevention programs in that they have shown little evidence of long-term effectiveness (Zigler, Taussig, & Black, 1992; O'Donnell, Cohen, & Hausman, 1991). This criticism may be unjustified due to the fact that Afrocentric violence prevention programs are relatively new, leaving little room to substantiate long-term effectiveness. Meta-analysis of the few appropriately designed evaluation studies found that few treatment programs for the serious and violent offenders have demonstrated large effect sizes. In addition, efforts to identify risk factors have outpaced our understanding of how to reduce the likelihood of beginning violent offending or reducing its persistence. Given that the development of treatment programs with high effect sizes is considerably more challenging than both the development of theories and identifying risk/resiliency factors for serious violent offenders, this is not surprising (Corrado and Peters, 2013).

Researchers accept that such programs have demonstrated some level of success at short-term decrease of violent behavior, modifying cognitive patterns supporting aggression, increasing social problem solving skills (Guerra & Slaby, 1990; Hammond, 1991), providing opportunity for positive and productive socialization into adult roles (Lee, 1987), providing cultural enrichment and life management, redefining manhood, and providing manhood training and teaching African values and principles (Cunningham & Mizelle, 1993; Nobles, 1989). However, very little is known in regards to the effect of such culturally relevant information and methodology on three major factors associated with violence and aggression; factors I refer to as the *Three Headed Dragon*. Depression, anger, and frustration are consistent across all host-related, environmental, and agent-related factors in the occurrence of assaultive violence. However, very little research has been done on culturally sensitive interventions aimed at reducing these factors in Black adolescent males (Baggio, 1987; Davies, 1989; Muran et al., 1989). Focusing on the effects of Afrocentric methodological approaches on level of depression, how anger is mediated, and on level of frustration tolerance may hold important keys to developing crucial treatment modalities for victims of violent experience as well as for those who perpetrate violence.

Epidemiological and etiological data on violence suggest that interventions should be designed to deal with the risks experienced by specific ethnic populations. Young African-American males face the greatest risk for violence in their circle of friends and acquaintances. Their anger, depression, and frustration become extremely dangerous, given the atmosphere of violence and self-hatred in which they find themselves. In their environments, all too often, ideas around respect take on delusional qualities where perceived slights can be extremely dangerous (Richardson and Robillard, 2013). These are issues that must be addressed in any therapeutic intervention. Anger, in particular, is something that the mental health field has historically failed to deal with in the general population (Braxton, 1992). Anger is seen as something that impedes treatment. This is particularly true if the subject is a young African-American male (as if young Black male anger cannot be tolerated let alone managed). I am reminded of a particular incident when working at an elementary school in the San Francisco Bay Area. I was working on contract basis for a program that specialized in providing educational services for emotionally disturbed children who were born into very difficult and unfortunate circumstances. While consigned to the elementary school I would provide counseling services for the children and at times, in-class support for the teachers. One particular morning I was summoned to a classroom where I was told a teacher was in a crisis situation with an active fight between two students. I turned my crisis intervention hat on and headed to the classroom. Fully prepared for blood and broken furniture, I stepped lively. When I arrived I was surprised to find that the "hot spot" was a 1st grade classroom! I arrived to find the teacher (a middle-aged Caucasian woman) in a panic and near tears as she struggled to keep two feuding little first-grader boys apart. One of the boys was near tears, the other refusing to cry. "What's going on?" I asked, not hiding my surprise at the small cadre of adults just outside the door and the almost comedic altercation inside the room. The teacher explained the boys started punching each other. She wasn't sure why. She and the rest of the children looked traumatized. For my part, I couldn't believe that the two pint-sized warriors could cause that much excitement. I immediately commanded that they both come with me. They both seemed to be breathing hard and one child near tears stepped out of the classroom willingly. The other child made it clear he wasn't going anywhere willingly. After seeing that I wasn't shocked by his expletives, I grabbed him by the arm and removed him from the classroom without too much fuss. Once outside the classroom the two started at each other; "He's going to hit me!" I replied, "He's not going to hit you," to which the other child chimed in, "I'm gonna bank on him!" "You're not going to 'bank' on anyone." I explained to him. He replied, "I'll bank on you!" to which I replied, "You won't be 'banking' on anyone today!" I then proceeded to pick the young warrior up, throw him over my shoulder while I held the more cooperative warrior's hand and walk with both of them down the hall to my office. As we started on our journey the uncooperative youngster flailed around and threatened that he was going to get his uncle to which I replied that he could "get his uncle, his momma, his grandmother, his whole family and we'll all talk about it". And furthermore, if he continued to act like a knucklehead, they all could watch me as I took my belt off and "whupped" his little behind! Of course, I had no intention of wielding a belt but he needed to know I meant business. Well, his protest was short-lived as we arrived at my office and they both entered. I sat them both down on the couch apart from each other. I gave them both a tissue and had them blow their noses and clean themselves up. I asked two questions, 1) why they were fighting? followed by 2) what they had eaten for breakfast? One child said he didn't know, the other claimed he had eaten cereal. We then discussed favorite cereals after which, I went into my lunch bag, took out my peanut butter and jelly sandwich, broke it in halves and gave each child a half. I could never be sure of what their breakfast routine was but they were both quite hungry. We discussed how the fight started (one took something the other had been using or something of that nature), how they were both friends before this, how they were sharing food as friends do, what they were going to play when they were allowed to go to recess and how their behavior affected the class. They were able to apologize and shake each other's hand at the end. I walked them back to the classroom and explained to the teacher that they were ready to return. The teacher did not thank me but told me that the principal needed to see me. Once I arrived at the principal's office, I was greeted with a discussion about Child Protective Services (CPS) being called. Quite naturally I was concerned about how I could help the situation whatever it was. I was floored when I learned CPS, had been called by the teacher who was at wits end and who had requested my help with the two little boys. The "belt" comment had earned me that honor, in her mind. Having been familiar with CPS reporting, I wasn't concerned. But as I pondered the absurdity of the situation, I thought about all the little Black boys who would be unnecessarily harmed by seemingly "well-meaning" teachers who had no idea what to do with them. The schematic she held for these two little boys was based on fear. The teacher was culturally out of her league. Her ignorance only matched her arrogance and both conditions were a detriment to those little boys. Evidence is clear that teacher expectation matters in the success of a child. Unfortunately, it was quite clear where this particular teacher expected these boys to be in ten years.

If part of the reason the individual comes to treatment is anger, then the treatment system is dysfunctional if the individual must cease to be angry in order to be treated. We must reconsider the system.

What I was engaged in with the little brothers at the elementary school, from a gang intervention perspective, is very much like (albeit on a much larger scale) the successful model utilized by the Violence Interrupters who operate in association with Cure Violence (aka CeaseFire). The Interrupters intervene in conflicts within Chicago, Illinois, in some of the most violent prone areas utilizing a community-based approach to preventing and reducing gang violence. Using the public health model as a framework, the program approaches violence as one would approach infectious disease by interrupting the next event or the next violent activity in an effort to prevent the spread of violent activity. This model prevents violence through a three-pronged approach (Skogan et al, 2008).

Detection and Interruption: Cure Violence is a data-driven model. Statistical information and street knowledge helps identify communities most impacted and provides a picture of those individuals at the highest risk for violence.

Behavior Change: Interrupters intervene in crises, mediate disputes between individuals, and intercede in group disputes to prevent violent events. Violence Interrupters work with members of the target population on the street, mediating conflicts between gangs and working to prevent the cycle of retaliatory violence from starting after a violent incident. Outreach workers are provided to counsel clients and connect them with services.

Changing Community Norms: Cure Violence/ Interrupters, through the use of public education and community-building activities, work to change the thinking on violence at the community level. Interrupters, also work at the street level providing tools for those most likely to be involved in altercations to resolve conflicts in other ways.

The participation of credible community members as outreach workers has been, no doubt, critical to the success of the Cure Violence program. This model represents a very promising community strategy for reducing violence and changing skewed social norms associated with violence.

Additionally, due to the stability of aggressive behavior patterns over time, there is a need for violence-reduction interventions for incarcerated youth. Most of the current programs were not developed to rehabilitate more hard-core, older adolescents whose behavior patterns may be too deeply ingrained to rely only on programs that focus on social skills. Indeed it could be argued that rehabilitation was never a goal for young Black men within the prison industry.

Marshall "Eddie" Conway, a former Black Panther and political prisoner, had been locked up since 1971. He was one of many former Black Panthers serving virtually life sentences largely the result of J. Edgar Hoover's COINTEL program. He had already brought his acute organizing skills to bear within prison, organizing a library and literacy program, earning three degrees, organizing a workers union as well as other human rights groups including Friend of a Friend. Over the years Eddie Conway had watched generations of young men come into the system; many behind the lure of the drug trade. He likened the drug trade to the same mechanism by which African children were lured onto slave ships with "red cloths" as he likened the criminal "justice" system to the new hold of the slave vessel. The Friend of a Friend (a phrase borrowed from the Underground Railroad) program formed an association with American Friends Service Committee around

2002 and has been extremely successful at mentoring Black men, transforming them and giving them a sense of purpose.

Friend of a Friend utilizes a curriculum developed by men who themselves have been involved in chaos and violence but who have made the conscious choice to move toward love and unity. Participants develop conflict resolution skills and develop mentorship relationships in prison and the relationships and skills extend to their communities as they return. Many of these young men have grown up without a significant male or father figure in their lives. And with the goal have having these young men leave the institutions operating at a higher and more mature emotional and intellectual level when they arrived, the program seems to be hitting the mark. The program exists in five prisons. Marshall "Eddie" Conway was freed on March 4, 2014, after 44 years in prison. He has always maintained his innocence.

In general, programs focusing on social learning, school-related behavioral problems, or reducing anti-social behavior have not been very effective for African-American youth in reducing violence. In the African-American community the number of victims of violent crime and the number of young African-American male offenders continue to increase. For African-American youth a different approach is needed. A comprehensive, culturally sensitive, and culturally relevant approach to violence prevention that will address the serious risk factors (poverty, physical and psychological changes in adolescence, male sex role and social expectations, differential access to power and history of exposure to violence) associated with violent, destructive behavior is indicated. Such a program would be one that is replicable and empowering for the African-American community, and which would take the curriculum out of the classroom and bring it to less traditional settings in the community, much like the above-mentioned programs. The program would be collaborative in nature and efficient in reaching a large number of high-risk youth in the community, and would acknowledge the existence of institutional sources of anger. It would reflect the *Muntu*—the totality of the human being as a spiritual energy/essence based entity. It would also acknowledge the tremendous impact of media on promotion and validation of violence, utilize media to present nonviolent alternatives to conflict, and would bring into operation a more cognitive learning theory model undergirded by an Afrocentric process and narrative with the aim of challenging and effecting a change in the ideas held to be true by the individual and the group as a necessary condition for behavioral change.

NOTE

1. Reggie is a pseudonym.

Chapter Eight

Cultural Relevancy in the Treatment of Symptomatology Related to Violence

There is an increasing call for the expansion of the knowledge base to improve violence prevention programming for young African-American males. This includes the development of conceptual frameworks as well as empirical research. In addition, in psychological and social services programming, there is an increasing call for cultural sensitivity to the needs of ethnic minorities in prevention and treatment effects (Cross, Bazron, Dennis, & Issacs, 1989).

TOWARD AN AFROCENTRIC FRAMEWORK

An Afrocentric framework allows for an Afrocentric conceptualization of the issues and problems related to violence, and an Afrocentric conception of the world, which permits the correction of falsifications. This is important historically in that, as the late anthropological historian Cheik Ante Diop (1991) states, "imperialism, which people of color all around the world have suffered under, is likened to a pre-historic hunter who first kills spiritually and culturally before killing physically" (pp. 1-2).

When I think of Diop's words, I am reminded, here, of the hit AMC network show, *The Walking Dead*, where roving bands of voracious zombies comb the land, mindlessly wandering, drawn by any signs of life. When they do find human life, they attack it, attempting to eat the flesh of the struggling victim until there is nothing left. If the victim survives she/he survives as a soul-less zombie, infected by the assault. Many cultures have fallen victim to the voracious predator that is Eurocentric imperialism. Those that survive, do so, long shorn of their cultural tether. They are chewed up and spit out as shells of what they once were... culturally and spiritually dead, as they become a part of the predatory march... void of spirit, in motion for the sole purpose of rabid materialism and consumption.

African-American people, in general, and young African-American males, in particular, suffer from a cultural void, which, for them, means spiritual death, in that culturally the two are inseparable. This negation of the history and intellectual realization of the African people is really a cultural and mental death, which preceded and prepared the way for acts of genocide here and elsewhere in the world.

One theory that has gained increasing support posits that part of the difficulty in effective functioning for young African-American males is that their spiritual psyche, and/or soul, and that of Africans, in general, has been killed by a deliberate falsification of their historical reality, destroying the foundation of reasonably human self-esteem (Akbar, 1986). This has paved the way for self-hatred and self-destruction. Nobles, Akbar, Wright, Azibo, White, Meyers, Parham and Kambon lead a cadre of pre-eminent social scientists who have called for restoration of the spirit. Restoring the spirit then, becomes a therapeutic necessity for young African-American males and in order to restore the spirit one must restore the history. This process can result in the restoration of self-esteem and a self-respecting consciousness out of which comes faith, hope, motivation, and intellect. These are all aspects that enable the individual to affect his/her environment and that serve as protective barriers or perceptual mediators to environmental factors that would normally result in feelings of anger, frustration, and depression.

FROM CONCEPTUALIZATION TO APPLICATION

A key question, then, becomes, how do we take the knowledge of African civilization and an African-based conceptualization of socio-historical issues and apply it to the discipline of psychology and to clinical practice in the treatment of factors or symptomatology associated with violent victimization and or behavior?

An important step in resolving this issue may be the recognition of the "African personality" itself. Azibo (1991) in his commentary on the development of a metatheory of African personality described the three most significant theoretical advances as follows:

(1) That African personality theory takes the Black perspective as the conceptual base for addressing the psychology of African people. This implies the use of cultural, historical, and conceptual analysis that employs and affirms principles that derive from the African social reality, and

(2) That African personality theory takes the position that personality has a biogenetic basis. In other words, there is an essence to human personality,

or to the nature of original human nature, that is spirit. This aspect is described as *the ontological principle of consubstantiation,* which posits that we are one people; we are of the same essence because this spiritual essence is somehow transmitted biogenetically at conception. (Nobles, 1986), and

(3) That African personality theory posits that there is a natural order of things. In other words, that order is an underlying principle upon which the cosmos and all therein operates.

Azibo further classifies three groups of theories having to do with African personality, along the paradigm of positivist (advanced theories, non-advanced theories), versus negativist pejorativist theories whereas Kambon proposed the categories of Afrocentric versus Non-Afrocentric as more appropriately capturing the distinguishing characteristics of these paradigms (Kambon, 1998).

Advanced theories (or Afrocentric models) are also known as formational theories and motivational product theories and incorporate all three of the advances referred to above. They are geared toward explaining directly the behavior or functioning of the African individual as a function of the state of his or her inherent African personality and any impinging environmental factors. What is interesting about these advanced theories is that they do not pay lip service to the three advances in African personality theory discussed. They are based on these advances, and, are therefore based in African worldview out of which grows explanations for the structure and development of personality, its underlying source of energy or motivation, its positions on psychopathology, and treatment.

Dr. Fu-Kia (1991) introduced many to the concept of the human being as a sacred entity—*Muntu*—an energy force that is revered throughout the life process. Drawing from the philosophy of the Bakongo people, he locates the *Muntu* within the context of a continuum connecting the world of the seen and the unseen. We rise as the sun upon our birth and join the ancestors at the sunset of our death. Dr. Fu-Kia explores the biogenetic basis of the individual (lendo kia tambukusu—"genetic power"), which is tied to the community as the community's "genetically bound rope (power)" the *N'singa dikanda waninga* is also revered, strengthening the connection between the living and the dead. It is this intricate quantum-physical relationship between the yet-to-be born, the newly born *Muntu* as it moves through life stages and the ancestral *Muntu* that forms the essence of who we are and the energy that drives how we unfold (Mbiti, 1970; Fu-Kia, 2003). For the Akan people, it is the *Okra* that represents this guiding spirit of man/woman, which is seen as being present before birth and continues after death (Abraham, 1962).

Dr. Akbar draws from the metaphysical principle of the *sunsum* as the basis of character; the moral sense that is indigenous to human beings which is foundational to the personality (Akbar, 1996). This is in contrast to the Western concept (Freudian-based) of moral conscience as a socially imposed construct. According to the Akan, the force of the *sunsum* can be shaped by experience, but as an implement of moral force, it is innate to the human being. Again, it is the spirit that drives this force and that forms the basis for our potential as human beings. African Psychology, according to Akbar, views the personality as purposeful in its emergence, harmonious with its ecology, and consistent with the laws of life.

In keeping with the expression of natural laws as expressed in African and Asian philosophical models, Akbar proposes three components of being that provide structure for the human species. All three components—the Physical, the Mental, and the Spiritual—are undergirded by the principle of self-preservation, as all life forms that are healthy adhere to the self-preservative process. Hunger, for example, is a drive that serves the process of self-preservation at a physical level. The mental sphere is a component whose effectiveness can be evaluated by the degree to which it is able to preserve and perpetuate itself. As the body experiences a natural hunger for food, the mind manifests a natural hunger for enlightenment. This hunger for knowledge is manifested early on in the trait or state of curiosity. It is indeed the normal state of affairs for a healthy infant to explore any and everything she/ he can get their hands, feet or mouth on. Later, increased mobility is powered by the desire to explore and know more. It is indeed, also opprobrium to our system of education that by the time these once-curious toddlers get to high school, many have all-but-lost this most important feature.

Finally, the survival orientation of the physical and mental spheres serve the ultimate purpose of spiritual survival. Both spheres act as vehicles for the transmission and growth of spiritual life. The hunger of the spirit, however, is a metaphysical hunger. The physical body hungers for food and water among other necessities and the mind hungers for knowledge whereas the spirit hungers for transcendence. And it is this drive, in the human being, that propels her/him toward goals higher than the material and higher than him/ herself (Akbar, 1996).

Nonadvanced theories are also known as transformational theories (or Transitional Afrocentric Models) and developmental process theories. Such theories of African personality primarily attempt to describe the process by which Africans develop a positive identity out of a negative denigrated and belittled African identity. These theories, though they do not purport to address personality per se, can be regarded within the conceptual framework of advanced African personality theory.

The third, and last, group of theories on the African personality that Azibo (1991) analyzed proceeds from Eurocentric conceptual bases, which are inherently anti-African. Deviance, deficiency, and notions of pathology characterize their formulations of African personality. These theories tend to conceptualize African pathology as normal and are derived from a Eurocentric conceptual base and an accompanying drive to maintain Caucasian over

Black status quo worldwide. Such models have also been referred to as "Pure Eurocentric" and "Pseudo-Africentric" models (Kambon, Bowen-Reid, 2010).

Advanced theoretical formulation of African personality would be the most likely choice in considering the development of treatment/intervention methodology for young African-American males, in that such theoretical formulation comprehensively addresses the interdependence of host and environmental factors on the development of personality and on the functioning of the African individual.

KEMETIAN FRAMEWORK

Another consideration for developing methodology for African Americans is that such methodology should be supported and structured by a framework that is itself Afrocentric. One of the most significant developments in Afrocentric psychology has been the awe-inspiring and eye-opening models and scientific discoveries that have emerged as a result of the research on ancient Africa and, in particular, on ancient Kemet (Egypt) (Amen, 1990; Karenga, 1990; King, 1990). Black people are inextricably tied to ancient Kemet, which holds keys for utilization of Afrocentric worldview in how a person conceives (1) man's relationship with man, (2) the relationships of man with the cosmos or nature, and (3) man's relationship with his Creator (Roberts, 1990). In his book *The African Origins of Civilization* (1974), Cheik Ante Diop writes,

> The oneness of Egyptian and Black culture could not be stated more clearly. Because of this essential identity of genius, culture, and race, today all Blacks can legitimately trace their culture to ancient Egypt and build a modern culture on that foundation. A dynamic modern contact with Egyptian antiquity would enable Blacks to discover increasingly each day the intimate relationship between all Blacks of the continent and the mother Nile valley. By this dynamic contact Blacks will be convinced that these temples, these forests of columns, these pyramids, these colossi, the bas-reliefs, mathematics, medicine, and all this science, are indeed the work of their ancestors and that they have a right and a duty to claim this heritage. (p. 131)

The ancient Kemetians developed and lived by a framework, which consisted of a set of interconnecting principles about the nature of the universe, the world, and humankind. For the ancients, the universal and human nature was constantly going through a process of life, death, and rebirth, and language both called forth and influenced the outcome of that process (Hardiman, 1990). Language was symbolic and all symbols had themes of the permanence of life (Carruthers, 1990; Nobles, 1986). The principles that made up this framework were as follows:

1. The principle of cosmic and social order, balance and harmony or Maat;
2. The principle of material and spiritual unity;
3. The principle of cyclic patterning;
4. The principle of complimentary dualities;
5. The principle of eternal rebirth; and
6. The principle of evocative language or Heka.

Dr. Hardiman (1990) writes that this framework, the ancient Kemetian (Egyptian) frame of reference:

> offers to African people a way of seeing and being in the universe that is positive, regenerating, and life sustaining, a way of seeing and being that provides images of truth and exemplary models of behavior which, if understood, internalized and applied to our present day reality, could help us eradicate some of the negative perceptions that block us from realizing our full potential as human beings, as men and women who grow from dialogical tensions generated by our complementary dualities. (p. 140)

Utilization of such a framework not only incorporates African world view, and the dynamics of African personality, but it offers a means of conceptualizing the "problem" of young African-American males along a time continuum or path. It informs the methodology in a way that allows for much more than the extinguishing of certain destructive behaviors. Such a framework allows for the development of methods that deal with deeper psychological issues that underlie problem behavior and encounter the African-American male on the path of life development. The stages of this path can be seen as occurring on four levels; (1) decomposition, (2) germination, (3) transformation, and (4) transcendence (Nobles, 1986). Again, to the ancient Africans, language was symbolic, full of signs and symbols. This is important in the development of treatment/intervention models that aim at affecting the attitudes, beliefs, and ideas of African-American males in an effort to impact behavior. We have previously addressed the connectedness of African-American people with the African worldview, the African personality, and the Afrocentric framework, which successful and advanced Black civilizations have operated from. The application of the history to the practice of psychology can be found in the signs and symbols, which have rules that need to be investigated. Our task as therapists can be seen as helping individuals to reclaim the path once they have gone off. Nobles (1986) outlines four keys, in relationship to signs and symbols, to serve in this effort. They are that: (1) there is imaging and energizing potential in the signs and symbols of ancient Africa; (2) there is an essential function that is always related to and represented by the signs and symbols; (3) the task of the therapist is to interpret those laws of being in the signs and symbols; (4) the signs help us to understand and identify what are the human possibility, probability, and potentiality.

The mandate for psychologists is to assist African-American males in addressing certain questions in the context of therapeutic intervention. What is their path? At what stage do they presently exist? What is their human potential? What is the meaning of their collective being? How do their perceptions create reality? Again, the task of the therapist can be seen as the task of changing the inappropriate behavior, which is, in effect, a task of culturally realigning the adolescent's behavior with Afrocentric principles of conduct, which are consistent with the highest level of human functioning. In other words, violent, self-destructive, and deviant behavior, which is based on culturally distorted ideas that offer little resiliency to states of depression and frustration, and destructive mediation of anger, must be realigned with culturally accurate and appropriate ideas which can lead to faith and hope in tomorrow, motivation to achieve, and intellectual development. Black IS as Black DOES. Many of our youth are not *DOING* Black. They are in fact operating on the basis of a Western European narrative. Dr. Nobles (2007) argues that their normal trajectory, based on fundamental African belief structures, has been "derailed" by the man-made disasters of colonialism and chattel slavery... and that this derailment was "intentional... the equivalent to "psychic terrorism in the form of civilizing, Westernization, modernity..." He believes derailment to be an important metaphor because like a train derailment, the train continues to move, albeit off its tracks. Black/African psychological and cultural derailment is difficult to discern due to the fact that Black/African life continues to move; however, in a direction that is off their developmental trajectory. The result is dehumanization, cultural genocide and the destruction of African general designs for living and interpreting reality.

They are operating from a set of characteristics (affectless-ness, individualism, competitiveness, control) that Akbar (1985) has described as culture-bound and prototypical to the white male. Furthermore, these characteristics are set within a European worldview ingrained with a massive orientation of patriarchy rising out of the "northern cradle" evolution of whites (Diop, 1978; Wobogo, 1976) which demands that the orientation to maleness be over-determined and that the dictates, which emanate from European cultural deep structure of separateness, independence, materialism, conflict, the imposition of order by the mightiest, and the incessant mastery and control of nature be pursued. These reflect the prominent patterns for interpreting reality within European worldview (Baldwin, 1985) and as such it can only promote and project its own image and selfish interests (Azibo, 1996). Black male violence and aggression operates from within this context.

It is important to note that it is not a given that young African-American males would automatically accept culturally relevant information. The MEE report (1992), *Reaching the hip hop generation*, found that many of the youth responding to the survey felt that identification with African culture further separated them from their peers. In the same report, Molefi Asante responded to the question of whether American urban street culture is compatible with African culture:

> Well, the rejection of Africa and the rejection of Egypt is part of what is wrong with these students. The fact that they did not respond in a positive way to African culture or Egypt shows how far the dislocation and the disorientation of the African-American has proceeded. The relationship to Africa emerges out of consciousness. The more conscious the students are, the more knowledgeable they are in terms of their cultural heritage and their ancestors; it also gives them a deeper sense of values. I think what we are seeing and experiencing is discontinuity, a detachment from values which is ultimately a detachment from culture. . . . I am not surprised that you find African-Americans on the streets who do not relate to African culture or who do not relate to Egypt; they have never heard these things in school, they have never seen them in a positive way on television, and the media does not give them any reason to have any attachment to it, so I would imagine that their values are dictated and reinforced by a Eurocentric perspective. (p. 30)

Many years later Asante's son would echo his father's sentiments. In his best-selling book, *Its Bigger than Hip Hop*, M.K. Asante Jr. recounts an interaction he had with a young eleventh-grader in the hallway at King-Drew High School in Los Angeles, just before delivering an address to the student body. It is worth recounting the story in its entirety here:

> She sat across from me and I noticed that her eyes, masked in blue contacts, wouldn't lift high enough to meet mine so I spoke first: 'Sup'. Her face, one half hidden behind tracks of strawberry-blond weave rose. 'Hi', she whispered, her eyes wandering... 'You reading that?' she chased. 'Yeah,' I said, glancing at the cover—*The Wretched of the Earth*—and offering her a look at the book. 'Here, wanna check it out.' She didn't budge, then finally—'I don't read nothin'. 'Nothing?' I asked to be sure. 'Nope, nothing. Less its for school' she confirmed. 'That's not cool, you know,' I said, not really knowing what to say. 'See, this book I'm reading right here is interesting because it breaks down a lot of information—information we should know as African Americans,' I said, to which she sprung a chuckle. 'What?' I questioned. 'What's funny?' 'African?' She quizzed. 'Yeah. African,' I said with a curious authority. 'I ain't African,' she swore. 'Where are your ancestors from, then?' I pushed back. 'I *dunno*, Europe or somewhere,' she said, straight-faced. I scanned her face, searching for signs she was just joking. She wasn't. 'African refers to our ethnic origin, American refers to our nationality, that's why I called you African-American.' 'I told you I ain't African', she snapped. I breathed as deeply as I my lungs would allow. 'Marcus Garvey said people who don't know their history are like trees without roots.' 'Who?' 'Marcus Garvey was a very influential and important Black man.' '*Umph*. I hate Black

people,' she said spitefully. 'Hate?' I said, shocked. 'Yeah, cause they ignor-ant. Not like white people—they sophisticated,' she explained to me. As I looked into the windows of Lisa's soul, I saw the eyes of Pecola Breedlove, the main character in Toni Morrison's 1970 novel *The Bluest Eye*. (Asante; 182-184)

When Eurocentrically-falsified African images are accepted as truth, such destructive images can be internalized and utilized by African-American youth, to structure their personalities, interpersonal relations, and value sys-tems. Such is clearly the case in the above story. The young lady represents a tragic loss of identity along with a skewed sense of self-worth and value. Her derailment (as the term is referenced above) represents a clear distortion in African Self Consciousness (ASC) as this conscious aspect of her personality finds itself "estranged from its natural condition under the 'unnatural' influ-ence of the European reality structure...that dominates American society" (Kambon, 2006). Still tethered to its core system, the African Self-Extension Orientation (ASEO), its role in defining the "African Survival Thrust" is certainly compromised leading to a quality of adaptation, which has proven unhealthy for the Black personality. The following explanation by Kambon should be clear:

> ...the crucial relationship between this construct and the phenomenon of Black mental health should also be clear. This is because the condition of "disorder" in Black personality occurs at the conscious level of functioning (at the level of ASC as opposed to the unconscious and deeply rooted ASEO level). In other words, where socialization and/or experiential indoctrinating processes are reflective of the alien (European) worldview (as is the psychological circumstance of most Africans in America today), to the extent that such a circumstance is experientially dominant in the life of the African individual (such as significant other in the form of persons or institutional processes), then the ASC is vulnerable to distortion or "Misorientation" by the alien/Eurocentric influences. When the alien worldview is also "anti-Black/anti-African" as in European American society where the dominant worldview is in fact the European Worldview (Baldwin, 1980a), then the nature of the distort-ing and misorienting influences on ASC become anti-African as well. (p. 98)

This condition extends to those within black communities who violently feed almost exclusively on those who resemble themselves and who share com-munity space with them. The Black-on-Black criminal, for example, is one who unknowingly internalizes White racist attitudes and beliefs, identifies them as his own and who subsequently acts them out. Amos Wilson (1990) explains this outcome: "The Black-on-Black violent criminal . . . is within a context that evokes criminal behavior which is not inhibited or redirected by effective opposing or alternative moral, intellectual, socioeconomic, cultural and valuational structures" (p. 83).

Akbar's (2003) classification system of mental disorders among African-Americans is consistent with Kambon's model. From a perspective of universal mental health, which includes the principle of self-preservation (survival thrust), the four classifications of disorders include (1) Alien-Self Disorders, (2) Anti-Self Disorders, (3) Self-Destructive Disorders and (4) Organic Disorders. Self-Destructive disordered persons, according to Akbar, are the most direct victims of oppression and those who perpetrate Black-on Black violence are certainly part of this grouping. These African-Americans are to some extent direct victims of Western/European racism and find themselves caught up in a vicious cycle of survival at any cost. Self-Destructive Disorders represent "self-defeating attempts to survive in a society that systematically frustrates normal efforts for natural human growth". Their mechanisms for survival end up so dubious and twisted (pimps, drug dealers, prostitutes, psychotics, addicts) that they find themselves engaging in behaviors that are self-destructive and equally detrimental to their own communities. Black-on-Black homicide and criminality, in this view, represents an acting out of the Self-Destructive Disorder. These individuals, like those in the other classes of disorders, have lost connectivity with the primary characteristics of their African Self-Consciousness.

In the MEE report (1992), Dr. Asante also discussed the fact that knowing about African culture centers young African Americans. If an individual does not know to whom he or she is connected in a historical sense, he or she will become disoriented, an individual who operates from a basis of confusion and illusion. Being centered through African culture can allow for attachment and, therefore, an abatement of disorientation and disconnectedness.

Dr. Nobles (2013) calls for the rescuing and reclamation of the African notions of "Sakhu Sheti/Djaer and Serudja Ta" as part of the disaster recovery strategy (which includes *man-made* disasters). Serudja Ta is described as a restoration process designed to "give reciprocal rebirthing to the African spirit."

> The idea of "Reciprocal Re-birthing" requires a mutually interactive application of African wisdom traditions, history, culture philosophy, and deep thought to illuminate, inform and develop simultaneously the re-birthing of (a) personal character (African personhood) and (b) environmental character (national sovereignty)... The ultimate charge in any recovery, treatment, intervention, and development process responding to the derailment of the African psychocultural moorings, that is, worldview by natural and/or man-made disaster, must be to make secure, set right, provide, fulfill, restore, repair, to make new again and to make grow, and flourish the authentic African spirit/humanity, ergo *Serudja Ta*." (Nobles, 254-255)

In conclusion, it should be noted that given the myriad consequences of cultural derailment, development of treatment methodology for young

African-American males is an extremely sensitive and challenging task. Young African-American males represent a significant portion of urban youth. Urban youth culture is characterized as an "oppositional culture" (MEE Report, 1992), and as a culture, is highly suspicious of messages perceived to represent mainstream culture. This poses a significant challenge for those who wish to disseminate information or ideas to this population through the use of popular media, i.e., television, film, music (radio), or Internet. Music videos, in particular, have been identified as possibly having the ability to be more current and to penetrate more quickly and completely than other forms of media, while maintaining an acceptance as part of the culture. In addition, music videos, via YouTube, Vimeo or that show up on Facebook, etc.... give the impression of being more shaped by the culture and are perceived as coming from within the culture, taking a role in defining the culture. Reflection on these factors could only enhance the development of future treatment methods.

Chapter Nine

Anatomy of a Study in the Real World: Changing Violent Outcome

THE EFFECT OF EXPOSURE TO CULTURALLY/HISTORICALLY
BASED MATERIAL ON LEVEL OF FRUSTRATION TOLERANCE,
LEVEL OF DEPRESSION AND MEDIATION OF ANGER IN
AFRICAN-AMERICAN YOUNG MALES

In addition to raising health and economic concerns, violence has had a tremendous impact on the social fabric of the Black community at large and on society as a whole. Still, addressing cognitive factors highly correlated with violent behavior has not been the focus of the nation's efforts to reduce violence among African-descended young men.

The following study was conducted to test the effectiveness of a brief group intervention, based on Afrocentric methodology, on level of frustration tolerance, depression, and mediation of anger in African-American young men. Initially, 20 subjects were pretested using the Reynolds Adolescent Depression Scale, Survey of Personal Beliefs, and the State-Trait Anger Expression Inventory. Fourteen subjects remained at the time of post-testing.

A repeated-measures ANOVA was performed on mean test scores for experimental and control groups. Also Cochran's C, Bartlett-Box F. and Box's M were conducted on pre- and posttest scores to evaluate the homogeneity of variance and normality.

While there was no significance found, qualitative trends indicate a reduction of depressive symptoms endorsed and reduction in level of state anger. As expected, subjects did not indicate an increase in their level of overall anger or an exacerbation of long-standing anger as a result of the intervention. A critical limitation of this study was the problem of small sample size, which compromised the assumption of homogeneity of variance and normality, affecting significance.

RESEARCH HYPOTHESES

1. Exposure to historically based/culturally relevant material will have a significant effect on level of frustration tolerance in young African-American males as measured by the Survey of Personal Beliefs (SPB).
2. Exposure to historically based/culturally relevant material will have a significant effect on level of depression in young African-American males as measured by the Reynolds Adolescent Depression Scale (RADS).
3. Exposure to historically based/culturally relevant material will have a significant effect on mediation of anger in young African-American males as measured by the State-Trait Anger Expression Inventory (STAXI).

Null Hypothesis

1. Exposure to historically based/culturally relevant material will have no significant effect on level of frustration tolerance in young African-American males as measured by the Survey of Personal Beliefs (SPB).
2. Exposure to historically based/culturally relevant material will have no significant effect on level of depression in young African-American males as measured by the Reynolds Adolescent Depression Scale (RADS).
3. Exposure to historically based/culturally relevant material will have no significant effect on mediation of anger in young African-American males as measured by the State-Trait Anger Expression Inventory (STAXI).

Methods

The purpose of this study was to test for the effectiveness of exposure to culturally relevant, socio-historically based material on level of frustration tolerance, on mediation of anger, and on level of depression in incarcerated young Black males with a history of violent behavior. There were important methodological issues to consider in doing this study. If the design was to be truly experimental, careful consideration had to be taken in the areas of procedure and participant recruitment. In addition, special care had to be taken to address issues of cultural relevancy in regards to the instruments and materials utilized. The attempt was made to select instruments with appropriate cultural representation within their norms. Currently there is a dearth of information on studies focusing on treatment that directly addresses cognitive factors associated with violence among young African-American males, which makes this study all the more critical. This chapter describes the program, methods, procedure, and measures used in this study. This section will introduce the program description, subject, experimental design, procedure, measures, and a brief discussion on the analysis of the data.

Population Description

The research for this dissertation was conducted at a correctional facility in a major Bay Area city. The facility is a non-secure residential correctional institution operated by the Juvenile Probation Department. The institution is located on the outskirts of an urban area, and serves juvenile males between the ages of fourteen and eighteen. The population normally averages from 90 to 110 residents and the institution has a capacity of 120.

The majority of residents are committed for felony level offenses, with many residents serving sentences for drug-related offenses and assaults. Lengths of commitment usually range from six months with these residents being furloughed to a transition house, to a year commitment, with seven months being the average length of stay. On average, the resident population is 61% Afro-American and 25% Latino, with the remainder of the population being Pacific Islander, Asian, and Caucasian.

The facility's program consists of four phases where residents must meet specific expectations in order to be promoted from one phase to the next. The phases are referred to as Step I (orientation), Step II (goal achievement), Step III (model resident), and Step IV (after care). Residents are required to complete a minimum of twenty-eight weeks on the first three phases. Time on these phases is extended when a resident violates a major rule. A resident's behavior is the determining factor as to the actual length of his commitment.

The facility's program is structured to include school, work details, recreational activities, and therapy groups. The county office of education administers a complete school program so that residents continue to earn high school credits during their commitment. Work details include assigned daily chores for each resident. Recreational and leisure activities are offered on a daily basis in both a structured format and as informal free time. Therapeutic groups revolve heavily around the issue of residents dealing with their criminal offenses, identifying how their victims have been affected, and changes they need to make in their behavior.

Participants

Thirty subjects ($n = 30$) were selected from a pool of incarcerated African-American youth between the ages of sixteen to eighteen years, with histories of violent and assaultive behavior. All subjects were residents of the host facility. The researcher announced the study in various classes conducted at the facility and asked that volunteers attend a specified orientation meeting. Only subjects who were able to meet the minimum requirement of availability for the eight-week treatment and testing period were selected for the study. Of the thirty subjects, twenty completed all testing instruments. Of the twenty subjects with completed protocols, ten were randomly assigned to the experimental group and ten were assigned to the control group. Participants were assigned three-digit code numbers strictly for identification purposes. Numbers in each age category were then selected and assigned to either a control group or an experimental group. The length of intervention was structured according to standards for brief therapy. The experimental group participants received twelve one to one and one-half hour sessions of exposure to culturally relevant/socio-historically based material and brief discussion of material presented. Both groups were pre- and post-tested.

One methodological issue in this study was the need to account for a small number of participants. The desired participant pool for this study was thirty, however, the participant pool depended on participant availability according to the facility's three- to six-month inmate cycle. Participants were chosen so that the entire participant pool would be available for the same five to eight weeks. Although an obvious choice for the study was to utilize one facility for control group and another for experimental group, there would certainly have been programmatic factors, differences in staff, general activities, and setting to account for.

Risk of identification was minimized by assigning code numbers. Test results did not affect the subjects' status as residents or their probation department cases. Test results served the sole purpose of this study, however, facility administration were given access to overall results of the study. In addition, a plan was developed to follow up control group participants by administering treatment to them.

Procedure

The researcher, after meeting with the teachers, visited each classroom announcing the study and the upcoming orientation meeting. Participants attended an orientation meeting conducted by the researcher, where they were introduced to the study. They were then asked to complete the RADS, SPB, and the STAXI. The participants were given an explanation of the study they were about to undergo, which included a clear explanation of their voluntary status as well as their right to withdraw their involvement in the study at any time. The researcher then thanked those potential participants who were not interested in participating and requested that they leave the room. This meeting took approximately two hours and included 1) an introduction which lasted approximately fifteen minutes, followed by 2) a testing session lasting approximately forty-five minutes, 3) a fifteen-minute break, 4) a testing session lasting approximately forty minutes and 5) closing remarks lasting approximately five minutes.

All subjects were then pretested according to schedule, after which testing instruments were collected and, later, scored. Three weeks after pretesting the experimental group subjects began the initial sessions, beginning with two one-hour sessions per day for the first two days, after which the participants received one session per day. The attempt was made to conduct two one-hour sessions per day in order to make efficient use of the subjects' available time. Subjects attended a one-hour session, after which they were given a 15-20 minute break. They were then called in (some had to be found) to begin the second session. It was felt that the time constraints of the facility made this necessary. However, the two-session structure seemed to negatively impact the subjects' ability to attend and concentrate on the material presented in the latter session. The sessions included approximately 45 minutes exposure to selected material in video, audio, or print format along with a 15-minute period of group discussion (see Appendix C). The control group subjects were allowed to follow their usual routine uninterrupted by the study. Throughout the study, participant withdrawal and incidents of participants being absent without leave (AWOL) became problematic. This accounted for the differing and reduced group sizes.

Within two and one-half weeks the experimental group completed twelve treatment sessions. The entire participant group (both control and experimental groups) was post-tested ten days later along the previous measures (RADS, SPB, and STAXI). Data was again collected and scored. Pre- and post-test data was then analyzed.

Measures

Several types of data were collected in this study. The Reynolds Adolescent Depression Scale provided information on depressive symptomatology. The Survey of Personal Beliefs provided information on irrational ideation in general and specifically on level of tolerance for frustration. The State-Trait Anger Expression Inventory provided concise measures of the experience and expression of anger.

REYNOLDS ADOLESCENT DEPRESSION SCALE

The Reynolds Adolescent Depression Scale (Reynolds & Coats, 1986) was developed as a measure of depressive symptomatology in adolescents. It is a useful choice in assessing the outcome of various therapeutic or educational interventions or in research where measuring adolescent depressive symptoms is necessary. This study makes no attempt at providing diagnosis of a specific depressive disorder, which would require a much more detailed and extensive evaluation. The RADS is a questionnaire, consisting of thirty sentences that ask examinees to describe feelings using a four-point Likert Scale-type format indicating how they usually feel. The RADS may be used for adolescents 13-18 years of age and is appropriate for group or individual administration. The RADS can also be administered orally to reading disabled adolescents. It may be hand or machine scored. The RADS is not designed to provide a diagnosis of specific depressive disorder.

Responses on the RADS are based on frequency of occurrence and are weighted from one to four points. Scores can range from 30 to 120 points and level of symptom endorsement associated with clinical depression is identified at or above 77 points.

The RADS offers high internal consistency as demonstrated by multiple measures of internal consistency (Kaplan & Kundert, 1988). The scale is quite robust showing strong content, criterion-related, and constructs validity. The high correlation's between the RADS and the related constructs of self-esteem, anxiety, loneliness, learned helplessness, suicidal ideation, hopelessness, and negative life events, social support, and hassles, support its convergent validity. Standardization of the RADS is based on sample size of 2,460 adolescents from grades 7 through 12, in a midwestern community. Since the original field-test the RADS has been administered to over 10,000 subjects with no significant difference in the data from the data in the original sample. Significant differences, however, were found for sex and grade but not for race. The separate norm tables provided for converting raw scores to percentile ranks across sex and grade should prove helpful in analysis of data for this study, given the age range of the participant pool. In addition, the cut of score for this instrument should help to illustrate the level and extent of depressive symptomatology in this special population. Information on the heterogeneity of the sample suggests that racial mix and the range of socioeconomic status are reflected in the norming of the test.

The thirty items in the RADS are designed to be easily understood, which increases its utility for adolescents. It has also been used as a screening measure for the identification of depressed adolescents in school settings. Given the dearth of appropriate depression-related assessment instruments specifically for inner-city African-American adolescents, the RADS is a responsible screening tool for this population. Further, clinical applications of the RADS support its clinical utility as a measure of depression in adolescents (Reynolds & Coats, 1986; Endicott & Spitzer, 1978).

THE SURVEY OF PERSONAL BELIEFS

The Survey of Personal Beliefs was developed as an assessment instrument for the endorsement of irrational ideation (Demaria et al., 1989). It is designed to assess the core irrational ideas of Rational-Emotive Therapy and to provide a measure of total irrational thinking. The instrument is a self-report test, which contains fifty items with five subscales and is scored in a six-point Likert-scale format. Higher scores indicate more irrational thinking.

The Survey of Personal Beliefs was chosen because it contains a subscale specifically designed to offer information as to what extent an individual possesses low frustration tolerance. The other four subscales (awfulizing, self-directed shoulds, other directed shoulds, and self-worth) were not applicable to this study. The instrument does not include the jargon of many inner-city Black youth, however, it reads easily and can be administered orally. The investigator assisted participants with items #7 and #34 during pretesting. When questions arose about these two items, the investigator repeated the questions aloud and offered the following transliterations:

Item #7: In some areas I absolutely should be more competent. Trans: There are some things in my life that I should, without a doubt, know more about.

Item #34: I can easily tolerate very unpleasant situations and uncomfortable, awkward interactions with friends. Trans: It's easy for me to cope in tough situations and when feeling at odds with friends.

The alpha coefficient reported for the test was .89, suggesting adequate internal consistency. In addition, a factor analysis was done to test the hypothesized factor structure. The test-retest reliability coefficients for the factors ranged from .74 to .87, which indicates adequate short-term temporal stability.

THE STATE-TRAIT ANGER EXPRESSION INVENTORY

The State-Trait Anger Expression Inventory was developed to provide concise measures of the experience and expression of anger. The instrument is the product of decades of research by Charles D. Spielberger and his associates and was developed as part of a long-term study of anxiety, anger and curiosity. An important distinction of this instrument is that it is based in a theoretical framework that distinguishes between anger, hostility and aggression as psychological concepts and that explicitly recognizes the state-trait distinction. This is an important aspect of the study, in that the field of mental health has traditionally not done well at dealing with the complex experience of anger in African-American men in general, and young African-American men in particular. It is also an important aspect due to concerns over raising or increasing the level of anger or angry affect in participants exposed to materials, which reveal harsh realities of racism and oppression.

The STAXI is comprised of forty-four items, which conceptually represents two domains: anger experience and anger expression. Anger experience is represented by two ten-item scales: State Anger and Trait Anger. The Trait Anger scale includes two four-item subscales: angry temperament and angry reaction. Anger expression is represented by three eight-item scales: Anger in (AX/In—holding in or suppressing angry feelings), anger-out (AX/Out—the expression of anger toward other people or objects in the environment), and anger control (AX/Con—the extent to which an individual attempts to control the expression of anger), and a total anger expression (AX/EX) score may be computed from the latter above mentioned three scales. The STAXI items are further grouped into three sections. Section I is comprised of the State-Anger items; Section II is comprised of the Trait-Anger items; and Section III is comprised of the Anger In, Anger Out, and Anger Control items.

The STAXI was chosen for its uniquely comprehensive assessment of the construct of anger and for its broad normative base. The STAXI manual reports norming for adolescents, college students, and adults. The normative data are based on administration to over 9,000 subjects, with Black students representing 18% of the adolescent participant pool. Percentile ranks are also available on male prison inmates, which may prove helpful for this study of incarcerated youth. Males and Females are reported separately for each norming sample. The median reliability reported for all scales is about .82. In addition there is evidence of both convergent and discriminant validity of the STAXI items (Biskin, 1988).

Analysis of Data

In order to determine differences in performance on the pretest and posttest, a repeated-measures analysis of variance (ANOVA) was performed on mean test scores from the pretest and posttest for the two groups: experimental and control.

For each research question, the descriptive statistics were determined for the pretest and the posttest for each of the groups. Also, Cochran's C, Bartlett-Box F, and Box's M were conducted on pre- and posttest scores to evaluate the homogeneity of variance and normality.

The analysis of covariance (ANCOVA) is a procedure used for comparing the treatment means that incorporates information on the quantitative variable x. The major assumptions in an analysis of covariance are that (a) the treatment's regression equations are linear in the covariable and (b) the linear regressions for the different treatments are parallel. The objective of an analysis of covariance is to compare treatment means after adjusting for differences among the treatments, due to the differences in the covariable levels for the treatment groups.

RESULTS OVERVIEW

Because the purpose of this study was to determine the effectiveness of a culturally relevant, socio-historically based intervention on African-American, delinquent, male juveniles incarcerated in a correctional facility, the design, instruments, and data analyses were selected to meet that end. Specifically, the study investigated the effect of the intervention on violence-prone adolescents' levels of depression (based on an assessment of depressive symptomology), endorsement of irrational ideation (as related to frustration tolerance), and experience and expression of anger.

The results of this study are organized under three research hypotheses as developed from a review of relevant literature.

HYPOTHESES

Hypothesis One

The first hypothesis is: Exposure to historically based/culturally relevant material will have a significant effect on the level of frustration tolerance in young African-American males as measured by the Survey of Personal Beliefs (SPB).

The null hypothesis is that the intervention will have no significant effect on the level of frustration tolerance of these subjects, at the .05 level of significance.

Pretest and posttest scores on the SPB for both groups, control and experimental, were collected and data were analyzed (see Table 1). The mean and standard deviation for the experimental group adolescents appeared to be remarkably reduced after the intervention; however, this result, unfortunately may have been due to the small sample size of $n = 14$. This would then be consistent with the results of the repeated-measures ANOVA. The results of the repeated-measures ANOVA, which did not show significant differences between groups over time (see Table 2), and a repeated-measures t-test conducted within the experimental group did not indicate that there was a significant difference over the two-and-a-half weeks' intervention.

The decision was to fail to reject the null hypothesis. Based on a review of the results of the statistical analyses, there were no significant differences found between and within the groups over time.

Hypothesis Two

The second hypothesis is: Exposure to historically based/culturally relevant material will have a significant effect on the level of depression in young African-American males as measured by the Reynolds Adolescent Depression Scale (RADS).

The null hypothesis is that there will be no significant difference between and within the groups over time. The descriptive statistics for the experimental and control groups at pretest and posttest are presented in Table 3.

The repeated-measures ANOVA shows significant differences between and within the groups and over time (see Table 4). However, the significant differences were found in both the control and experimental groups. The reduction in the level of depression may be due to a variety of factors and therefore, cannot be solely attributed to the culturally relevant intervention designed for this study.

The null hypothesis of no significant difference in level of depression can be rejected. However, ANCOVA results do not confirm that PRERADS is a significant predictor of POSTRADS, regardless of group (experimental or control).

In Figure 1, the significance level of 0.355 for the GROUP variable indicates that experimental group POSTRADS adjusted for the covariable PRERADS is not significantly different from the corresponding response for the control group.

Table 9.1. Descriptive statistics for the Survey of Personal Beliefs (SPB), Pretest and Posttest, for the Groups: Experimental and Control

	Group				
	Experimental			Control	
	($\underline{n}$ = 6)			($\underline{n}$ = 8)	
Test	$\underline{M}$	$\underline{SD}$		$\underline{M}$	$\underline{SD}$
Pretest	34.67	10.25		31.75	4.03
Posttest	30.50	5.36		29.63	3.78

Table 9.2. Summary Table of Repeated-Measures ANOVA Performed on Mean Test Scores from the Survey of Personal Beliefs (SPB) Pretest and Posttest between Groups.

Source of Variance	df	SS	MS	F
Between Subjects	13	617.00		
Groups	1	24.65	24.65	0.05
S(G)	12	592.35	49.36	
Within Subjects	14	364.86		
Test	1	67.86	67.36	2.81
Group x Test	1	7.15	7.15	0.31
Residual	12	289.85	24.15	
Total	27	981.86		

Hypothesis Three

The third hypothesis is: Exposure to historically based/culturally relevant material will have a significant effect on the mediation of anger in young African-American males as measured by the State-Trait Anger Expression Inventory (STAXI).

The null hypothesis is that there will be no significant difference between and within the groups over time.

Mediation of anger was operationalized to include selected subscales of the STAXI: Situational Anger Scale (SANG), Trait Anger Scale (TANG), Temperament Anger Scale (TANT), Angry Reaction Scale (TANR), Anger Expression In Scale (AXIn), Anger Expression Out Scale (AXOut), Anger Expression Control Scale (AXCon), and the compiled (the sum of AXIn, AXOut, and AXCon) Anger Expression Scale (AXEx). Each of the subscales listed was analyzed separately and the results follow.

The SANG

There appeared to be higher levels of dispositional anger or anger toward their situation (the attitudes measured by the SANG) in the experimental group subjects (see Table 5). Their scores were lowered at posttest, indicating lowered levels of situation anger. However, the control group's scores on the SANG were significantly lower at the .05 level than the experimental group's at pretest (see Table 6), and they were increased after the two-and-a-half weeks' period.

Table 9.3. Descriptive Statistics for the Reynolds Adolescent Depression Scale (RADS), Pretest and Posttest, for the Groups: Experimental and Control

	Group				
	Experimental ($\underline{n}$ = 6)			Control ($\underline{n}$ = 8)	
Test	$\underline{M}$	$\underline{SD}$		$\underline{M}$	$\underline{SD}$
Pretest	74.17	8.33		81.75	6.56
Posttest	69.00	6.32		75.75	8.83

The significant difference detected with the repeated-measures' ANOVA was due to differences between the groups at pretest. These groups were not equivalent initially. The results of the analyses on the SANG indicate that the null hypothesis should not be rejected for the anger as measured by this subscale.

Trait Anger or the tendency toward maintaining angry feelings or chronic anger, as measured by the TANG, *Temperament Anger* or the tendency toward a "quick temper" and the lack of impulse control with respect to angry behaviors, as measured by the TANT, *Angry Reactions* or the tendency toward sensitivity to negative evaluations by others, as measured by the TANR, scores on the *Anger Expression Scale*, which measures the tendency with which angry feelings are held in or suppressed, as measured by the AXIn, how often an individual expresses anger toward other people or objects in the environment as measured by the AXOut, and how often an individual attempts to control the expression of anger as measured by the AXCon, as well as scores on the compiled anger expression scale, the AXEx were fairly consistent between groups over time. There were no significant differences as determined by the repeated-measures ANOVA. The short-term intervention did not and was not expected to affect trait anger and anger expression. Therefore, the decision was to fail to reject the null hypothesis for all the above.

DISCUSSION

This study sought to determine whether exposure to audio/visual and print material reflecting cultural relevancy and socio-historical perspective would impact cognitive factors highly correlated with violent/deviant behavior. Of primary concern were the presence and/or level of impact of the designed

Table 9.4. Summary Table of Repeated-Measures ANOVA Performed on Mean Test Scores from the Reynolds Adolescent Depression Scale (RADS) Pretest and Posttest between Groups

Source of Variance	df	SS	MS	F
Between Subjects	13	1223.61		
Groups	1	352.19	352.19	4.85[a]
S(G)	12	871.42	76.62	
Within Subjects	14	741.37		
Test	1	213.76	213.76	4.87[a]
Group x Test	1	1.19	1.19	0.03
Residual	12	526.42	43.87	
Total	27	1964.98		

[a] $p < .05$

intervention on the cognitive factors of depression, frustration tolerance, and anger. The study's findings provide some qualitative support for use of a brief therapeutic intervention, developed out of an Afrocentric methodological base, on cognitive factors correlated with violent, self-destructive, and deviant behavior. Currently there is little information on studies focusing on culturally relevant treatment strategies addressing such factors in young men of African descent. This makes the subject study all the more critical. The tested intervention was designed to do more than impact destructive behaviors. It was designed to deal with psychological issues underlying the behavior, motivating discussion around the following fundamental questions:

1. At what stage do they presently exist?
2. What is their human potential?
3. What is their path?
4. What is the meaning of their collective being?
5. How do their perceptions create reality?

In doing so, evidence of cultural realignment of the participants' negative and destructive attitudes and beliefs with culturally accurate and appropriate ideas and beliefs, was apparent. For example, an indication of initial negative attitudes and beliefs was the high level of intolerance for the views of their peers. Participants would respond to other group members by making statements like, "Shut the fuck up!" "Man fuck that!" or "You don't know shit." Participants would argue excessively. Also participants would rap or reiterate the lyrics to rap songs condoning and glorifying Black-on-Black violence,

Model Summary a,b						
	Variables				Adjusted	Std. Error of the
Model	Entered	Removed	R	R Square	R Square	Estimate
1	PRERADS. GROUP c,d		.473	.224	.083	7.9766

a. Dependent Variable: POSTRADS

b. Method: Enter

c. Independent Variables: (Constant), PRERADS, GROUP

d. All requested variables entered.

ANOVA[a]						
Model		Sum of Squares	df	Mean Square	F	Sig.
1	Regression	201.829	2	100.915	1.586	.248b
	Residual	699.885	11	63.626		
	Total	901.714	13			

a. Dependent Variable: POSTRADS

b. Independent Variables: (Constant), PRERADS, GROUP

Coefficients[a]								
		Unstandardized Coefficients		Standardized Coefficients			95% Confidence Interval for B	
Model		B	Std. Error	Beta	t	Sig.	Lower Bound	Upper Bound
1	(Constant)	54.132	25.686		2.107	.059	-2.403	110.668
	GROUP	-4.745	4.916	-.293	-.965	.355	-15.565	6.075
	PRERADS	.264	.312	.257	.847	.415	-.423	.952

a. Dependent Variable: POSTRADS

Figure 9.1. Analysis of covariance results for experimental and control groups where dependent variable is posttest Reynolds Adolescent Depression scale and covariate is pretest Reynolds Adolescent Depression scale.

referring to women as "bitches" and black men as "niggers/niggas." Around midway through the intervention the participants began to question what they were saying by repeating these lyrics, who was pushing this type of destructive rap music, and why. By the sixth session participants began to show a change in group movement and expression of group unity. They began to become more interactive and to develop a sense of ownership and defensiveness for the project. For example, on occasion when interrupted by a staff member the group members would become angry and say things like, "They

Table 9.5. **Descriptive Statistics for the State Anger Scale (SANG), Pretest and Post-test, for the Groups: Experimental and Control**

	Group				
	Experimental			Control	
	($\underline{n}$ = 6)			($\underline{n}$ = 8)	
Test	$\underline{M}$	$\underline{SD}$		$\underline{M}$	$\underline{SD}$
Pretest	26.67	9.46		17.38	4.07
Posttest	23.50	5.32		19.38	4.24

always wanna fuck something up. This is *our* shit!" Also, experimental group members were initially reluctant to be on time and were clearly preoccupied with their daily interactions at the facility. This changed as they began to show more interest in the information presented.

Although it is difficult to measure the construct of spirit using empirical methods, this study attempted to offer a structured format for restoring the spirit, which in turn was expected to impact the subject's self-respecting consciousness. This self-respecting attitude is essential in developing a reasonable foundation for self-esteem (Akbar, 1986). It was expected that differences in the level of depressive symptoms endorsed between control and experimental groups would indicate a noticeable impact on the participants' level of self-respecting consciousness. Half the experimental group participants showed strong differences in critical items endorsed across pre- and post-testing on the RADS. For example, item #14 indicating self-harm or suicidality: "I feel like hurting myself," was endorsed pretest as 2 (Hardly Ever), 3 (Sometimes), and endorsed posttest as 1 (Almost Never). Item #26: "I feel worried," was endorsed pretest as 3 (Sometimes) and posttest as 1 (Almost Never) and 2 (Hardly Ever). All the experimental group members endorsed a critical self-efficacy item: "I feel like nothing I do helps anymore," pretest as 4 (Most of the time), 3 (Sometimes), and 2 (Hardly Ever), and posttest as 1 (Almost Never), with one exception of 2 (Hardly Ever). These trends were not surprising given Akbar's description of the role of *historical reality* and the impact of its destruction on people of African descent in general (Akbar, 1986). Support for the intervention's impact on motivating cognitive processes which serve as protective barriers to environmental factors that normally result in increased levels of anger and depression, although not *statistically significant*, was evidenced by RADS and STAXI results. When examining individual RADS scores we find a notice-

Table 9.6. Summary Table of Repeated-Measures ANOVA Performed on Mean Test Scores from the state Anger Scale (SANG) Pretest and Posttest Between Groups

Source of Variance	df	SS	MS	F
Between Subjects	13	723.29		
Groups	1	308.58	308.58	8.94[a]
S(G)	12	414.71	34.51	
Within Subjects	14	470.51		
Test	1	2.33	2.33	0.07
Group x Test	1	45.76	45.76	1.30
Residual	12	422.42	35.20	
Total	27	1193.80		

[a] $p < .05$

able group difference in the number of participants who move from a score *well* above the cutoff score for serious depression to a score below that of the cutoff. Pretest scores for experimental group indicate a total of three participants who score above the cutoff while control group scores indicate five participants scoring above the cutoff score. However, posttest results reveal that one of six experimental group members scored in the critical range for serious depression, whereas seven of eight control group members scored in the critical range for serious depression.

Nobles' (1986) notion of *path of life development* and the subsequent stages ((1) decomposition, (2) germination, (3) transformation, (4) transcendence) associated with this path were useful in establishing a framework for this intervention. The former three stages were utilized. The decomposition related material was expected to produce results including the expression of anger and surprise as well as amusement and disgust. When viewing this material, which offered a history of past and current negative images and myths about people of African descent, participants reacted immediately. They responded overwhelmingly with anger and a sense of injustice.

The stage of germination was a crucial one for this study. It was hoped that the participants would begin to challenge some of their negative perceptions through this stage. Their response to the germination-related material was one of interest. They expressed surprise and wonder at hearing about a history of the Moors. Their response to the videotapes was notable. They seemed to notice the way the speaker dressed and then the amount of gold or jewelry the speaker wore. Finally, once the information was presented, the participants displayed their sense of pride at what was being said. The groups' exclamations include: "Tell it!" "That fool's got game!" and "Damn, he's deep!" In addition, they showed germinating signs of recognizing African pictures and artifacts and objected when shown a video segment that misrepresented historical facts. They verbally expressed their anger and were able to cite information introduced earlier in the study.

The stage of transformation attempted to challenge culturally distorted ideas about themselves and to begin to realign their thinking with Afrocentric principles. Changes were noted in three broad areas during this stage: (1) in their level of attention during sessions, (2) in their verbal responses, (3) in their within-group behavior. By the ninth session, earlier problems with attentiveness were negligible. Even where participants had the most difficult time with attention to audiotaped information, their attempts were visibly noticeable. Group members at this stage would attempt to keep each other quiet. When seeing the gold artifacts and symbols in ancient Kemet they responded immediately with amazement. They also expressed amazement at seeing black people all around the world. They began to verbally associate their love for gold with their ancestors, as they discussed their gold teeth and jewelry. Participants paid particular attention to the Minister Farrakhan videotape, which featured speakers who challenged the destructive actions of black youth, some of which the group members had participated in. They began to laughingly joke about different speakers saying things like: "He's fat!" "Look at that hair!" and "Damn, he's pissed." Then, in more serious tones, they expressed their agreement with the speakers saying, for example, "Niggas need to chill on all that violence." "You know they right!" "You know that shit is real" (You know they are telling the truth). In addition, their level of energy seemed to increase, as did their willingness to discuss the material. As a group, we experienced fewer unplanned breaks, and they began to raise interesting questions and comments regarding their anger at never having learned this information in school. Some discussed going to school once they are able to leave the institution, and others discussed simply not returning to be institutionalized.

All three stages combined to attempt to change participants' attitudes and/ or understanding of their individual situations. These goals were appropriate for the use of a short-term cognitive approach where specific cognitions (thoughts or images) or schemata (silent assumptions) account for the onset and persistence of symptoms (Ursano & Hales, 1986).

This brief therapeutic intervention was directed at addressing the early stage objectives for cognitive therapies (Ursano & Hales, 1986). Participants were made aware of stereotyped views they bring into situations. For example, participants initially came into the sessions identifying themselves as "gangsters, gangsta-macks, criminals, and straight villains." They seemed to be quite proud of their self-proclaimed "mobster" status. They were made to recognize and adjust such views, in order to consider a more objective reality. They were also made to identify schemata responsible for their thinking and behavior. An example of the information utilized to redirect their cognitions was the print material by the late social scientist, Amos Wilson, who expands on the term *schemata* to include not only personal schemata but social-societal schemata and its role in supporting negative assumptions, ranking behavior (Sapolsky, 1989), and acquisition of status. Another example of information used for this purpose was material from *Pipe Dream Blues* by Greg Lusane (1991), which offers objective data on arrests, prosecution, and imprisonment of youth by race.

Although this therapeutic intervention was designed with specific timelines it is important to note that there was a degree of flexibility built into treatment duration. The investigator had to deal with participants' disruptions at times during the earlier sessions. For example, during one session an argument ensued between two participants over an ongoing issue between them. Most participants were drinking coffee, and during the course of the argument paper was thrown back and forth and then coffee from the cups of the two participants. Some of the coffee was thrown on the researcher and the session was discontinued. Even an act as simple as bringing donuts into the session for participants proved to be a challenge. Initially, the participants would storm the donuts in an almost frenzied attack. The act of obtaining the donuts became an issue of power and control. Later, the researcher learned that the participants were holding the donuts to return to their dorms, where they would use them to barter or gain favor with other inmates. The researcher had to set strict rules and limits about how the participants could help themselves to the donuts, in order to ensure equitable distribution. In addition, the probation department requested that the researcher establish protocol to discontinue the practice of carting donuts off to the dorms.

The sessions were also affected by overall operational problems at the facility. At times there were delays in getting the participants to the sessions on time, due to problems that occurred the night before or due to various crises. Also, there were delays due to room changes and subsequent technical difficulties with audio-visual equipment. Certainly these distractions served to reduce the participants' ability to focus on the material presented which could also be a factor in the level of significance. A *time limited attitude* (Binder, Henry, & Strupp, 1987) was adopted to maximize therapeutic gain and efficiency given the relative instability of the process within this institution.

Leventhal's perceptual-motor theory was useful in conceptualizing an agency for impacting the operational feelings and memories responsible for producing attitudes about, and evaluations of, anger inducing events in their immediate surroundings, which had led to incarceration. Leventhal's third contributing mechanism to the experience of emotion is the mechanism of conceptual processing (Leventhal & Mosbach, 1983), which views anger as a subjective perceptual experience that can be modified, thereby modifying the individual's experience of anger and relative depression. An interesting aspect of the study was its impact on state (or situational) and trait (chronic) anger. There were no overall significant differences between control and experimental group experiences of anger. It is quite possible that this lack of significance, along with the element of distraction, was connected to the issue of time. Perhaps the level of cognitive processing required to produce a significant reduction in state anger might be a function of cognitive rehearsal. Possibly, the time allotted for the intervention was not sufficient to evidence change from pre- to post-testing. As expected, exposure to the intervention material did not cause experimental group members to increase their suppression or expression of anger, nor did exposure to the material exacerbate longstanding anger. The study also found a general trend of decreased intensity of angry feelings in participants who received the intervention. Those participants who did not receive the intervention showed a slight increase in intensity of angry feelings with a wider variance between pretest and posttest scores. Perhaps this decrease can be partly explained by considering that the existing feelings of anger within these youth are only exacerbated by their institutional experience and by not feeling understood by institutions (criminal justice, education, etc.) or by those in authority. Perhaps feeling understood, obtaining a historical perspective on their behavior, and being offered direction and a path in their life may indeed aid in the regulation of motor responses by changing the participants' attitude or understanding of threat-inducing situations, resulting in the removal or reduction of perceived threat that normally accompanies anger.

PRIMARY RESEARCH HYPOTHESIS

The first research hypothesis, exposure to historically based/culturally relevant material will have a significant effect on level of frustration tolerance in young African-American males as measured by the Survey of Personal Beliefs, was rejected, accepting the null hypothesis of no significant effect.

There were several factors that may have contributed to the finding of no significance for effect on level of frustration tolerance. Issues surrounding the participants' relative level of competency for this instrument were anticipated, due to the head teacher's report of a wide variation in reading levels. Although the researcher was available for interpretation and assistance in reading of test items (see methods section), the test length proved to be problematic. The result was an increased tendency for malingering. Four of the fourteen SPB protocols had to be considered potentially invalid due to random responses or items that were skipped. Most of these problems could have been eliminated by isolating the ten-item low frustration tolerance scale and orally administering these items. The frustration tolerance scale is not difficult to administer, and the items were not difficult for this population to understand. The SPB evaluates irrational cognitions and cognitive styles, which produce frustration in social settings. It is able to offer information as to what extent an individual possesses low frustration tolerance. Increasing sample size and/or even sample sizes would not have solved for test-taking issues but would have resolved problems with homogeneity and level of significance strength. In addition, the nature of confinement itself may call for a certain level of frustration tolerance, which may have accounted for scores in the normal range for this instrument.

The second research hypothesis, exposure to historically based/culturally relevant material will have a significant effect on level of depression in young African-American males as measured by the Reynolds Adolescent Depression Scale (RADS), was rejected. However, even though lack of homogeneity, due to small sample size, greatly compromised the generalizability of this finding, the interventions' effect on the depression variable, for reasons previously stated, was apparent. Still another set of factors, which must be ruled out are the possibility of transference/counter-transference effects. It must be noted that some of the change in depressive symptomatology endorsed may have been due to the race, age, style and general presence of the researcher. Perhaps having ongoing visits or dialogue with someone from the outside could have been sufficient to promote such a change in scores.

The third research hypothesis, exposure to historically based/culturally relevant material will have a significant effect on mediation of anger in young African-American males as measured by the State-Trait Anger Expression Inventory (STAXI), was rejected and the null hypothesis of no significant effect was accepted. All of the anger mediation indices showed no significant effect. The state anger index showed a trend where intensity of angry feelings tended to decrease in experimental group participants. Thirty-seven percent and five tenths of control group participants showed a reduction in state anger as compared to 50 percent of experimental group participants. In addition, experimental group scores on state anger were reduced by a total of 38 points whereas control group scores were reduced by a total of 15 points.

Assessing how one mediates anger or angry feelings is probably a more in depth process than one instrument can satisfy. Although the STAXI may accurately offer a view of one's cognitive style in handling anger, certainly there are other indicators that could successfully be used adjunct to this instrument. Self-reports, observational reports, as well as behavioral indicators could, if used together, support testing on mediation styles.

CLINICAL IMPLICATIONS

Differences in pre- and posttest depression scores suggest an impact on participants' sense of perceived powerlessness, which, if internalized, leads to depression. The risk for increased anger expression and acting-out behavior as a result of exposure to treatment, were minimal. This has strong implications for use of such material in educational and mental health arenas where identity formation and an individual's sense of self are socially driven. These findings underscore the importance of positive imagery in the development of African-descended youth, suggesting the possible clinical relevancy of rites of passage programs. The potential for effective treatment of delinquent or incarcerated young men of color, using exposure to similar material or culturally-based programs, seems to be quite strong. Both the efficiency and cost-effectiveness of this brief group-therapy design has wide implications for the field of mental health as well as for the development of crime and violence prevention programs. Finally, this study makes a strong case for the inclusion of Afrocentric methodology and the development of culturally-sensitive models in the discussion of violence prevention and intervention among African-descended people. The participant population for this study may very well be one of the most difficult populations to work with in the field of clinical psychology. Many of the young men who are incarcerated at this level have already internalized much of the destructive and negative imagery put forth by this society about them. Many of these young men were faced with a dilemma similar to that described previously by the researcher and made decisions that placed them in custody. They represent the fruition of the destructive value of such imagery as well as of their socio-economic reality. Still, this intervention model, based on Afrocentric methodology, which includes an Afrocentric understanding and conceptualization of their "problem," was able to produce noticeable change in important cognitive areas. Perhaps further study of the impact of interventions of this type on cognitive-emotional factors associated with violent behavior would reduce the need to wait on behavioral outcome as primary means of evaluation; a time when, for some youth, it is too late.

LIMITATIONS OF THE STUDY

This study was a difficult one. It was plagued with problems of logistics. Conflicts between the probation department and the education department posed problems for the researcher. Although education administration showed interest in the study, the teaching staff seemed divided in their level of caution and concern regarding the study. The researcher had met with the teachers formally and had announced the study in each of their classrooms.

Therefore, their level of caution was not anticipated. One problem this caused was that participants were not always available at the onset of the therapy sessions. At times, the researcher had to actually visit the respective classrooms (pulling the participants out) and explain to the teacher (or substitute) that the student was needed for the session.

Problems with the probation department had to do with issues of control over participants, access to rooms and to equipment, and communication with the education department. The probation department, for example, was responsible for getting inmates to and from breakfast and for delivering information about who was to be excused for the study each morning. Miscommunication at this level made it extremely difficult to obtain the appropriate participants in a timely manner in the beginning. In addition, locations were not always consistent. On the first day, the probation staff did not seem to know about the study, let alone have a room set up and available for it. Problems with the facility's video equipment posed serious time delays as well as difficulties in transitioning from print to video material. The room the study was assigned to, initially, was problematic in that it was too large and had large windows, which faced the courtyard and the dorms. Other inmates would float by at times and peer into the windows, knock on the windows, and/or shout to participants. This proved to be extremely distracting for both the researcher and participants. The study did not take precedence over other staff priorities, and time had to be allowed for disciplinary problems and consequences with experimental group participants. Behavioral problems were anticipated and occurred on an ongoing basis towards the beginning of the study. Group members would shout obscenities and threaten each other routinely.

Working within the criminal justice system and being from the outside was, at times, disadvantageous in that communication between the researcher, probation, and education was not always clear. Expectations, at times, also required further clarification. Overall, however, the staff and students were glad to have the study. Behavior management was certainly a role the researcher had to assume during the first half of the intervention, as participants would test limits and attempt to "get over" or take advantage of the researcher's lack of familiarity with particular rules and procedures.

When considering generalization of findings to the total population of young African-American males, one must be careful to take into consideration breadth of experience among young African-American males. Although young African-American males share many of the same experiences and stressors given the inherent racism in American society, they tend to differ across class lines, cultural orientation, and familial stability. Participant selection, methodology, and experimental procedure might attempt to solve this problem by minimizing the level of variance of experience and socioeconomic difference.

One methodological issue in this study was the need to account for a small number of participants. The desired participant pool for this study was thirty, however, the participant pool depended on participant availability according to the facility's three to six month inmate cycle. A major challenge was that participants had to be chosen so that the entire participant pool would be available for the same five to eight weeks. Although an obvious choice for the study was to utilize one facility for control group and another for experimental group, there would certainly have been programmatic factors, differences in staff, general activities, and setting to account for. Within one institution there could be participant exposure to programs that might contribute to changes in dependent variables or co-factors.

One limitation of this study was the problem of small sample sizes. Both experimental and control groups began with fifteen members for a total of thirty participants. Ten participants had to be eliminated immediately due to incomplete testing. Later, both groups were reduced due to drop out and AWOL (absence without leave) incidents. As a result although both experimental and control groups began with appropriate numbers, the overall number of participants towards the end of the study was not enough to avoid violating the assumption of homogeneity of variance and normality. Although an exhausting analysis of the data was conducted, using both ANOVAs and ANCOVAs, no significance was found relative to the tested hypotheses.

Participants' test-taking styles were also problematic. Evidence of malingering was found in some of the SPB results. This could have been eliminated by lowering the number of items (fifty) isolating the ten-item low frustration tolerance scale and administering only these items. The SPB was designed for a level of literacy beyond some participants (8th grade reading level). Additional oral administration, including definitions of descriptive words, may have solved problems of accuracy for some, where participants may have been too embarrassed to ask about terms they found difficult. These problems resulted in the inability to accurately detect changes in the low frustration tolerance scale. In addition, low frustration tolerance was a difficult construct to measure. Perhaps the addition of observational reports or an item checklist would have been useful in determining the participants' level of frustration tolerance. In addition, screening for Attention Deficit Disorder would have aided in the selection of participants. One of the experimental group participant's early departures brought a sense of calm to the group. Prior to leaving he had been extremely disruptive and showed a distinct inability to attend or sit in one place for any length of time. Later it was found that this participant was on medication. This information would certainly have been beneficial in the selection process.

Another possible limitation of this study was that the pre- and posttest differences may have been minimized, thereby reducing effect size. Although confidentiality was requested, the potential for communication between experimental and control group participants existed. Therefore cross-contamination certainly could have occurred.

The method of evaluation may also have been a possible limitation. It is possible that a more qualitative investigation of the desired constructs may have been valuable in measuring change. Perhaps critical changes in violent antecedents and outcome occurred that were not detected by the instruments chosen.

Finally, a strong limitation to this study was the lack of funding for its design and implementation. Proper editing of the material presented would have minimized delays in transition from audio to audio-video material presented. Editing would have allowed the merging of musical selections with visual images, possibly reducing problems with attention and focus in experimental group participants.

Funding could certainly enhance the design by expanding the study to include several like institutions thereby increasing sample size, adding research assistants to meet the intervention demands, technical assistance and the expansion of assessments to include more qualitative and behavioral assessments.

SUGGESTIONS FOR FURTHER RESEARCH

An important issue relative to this study is whether the inclusion of culturally relevant, socio-historically based materials in mainstream therapies could prove efficacious for young African-American men, in particular and African-Americans in general. This question certainly is one that deserves a closer look. Results of this study were profoundly limited by the choice of evaluation parameters (quantitative versus qualitative), dynamics between the subsystems at the study site, and sample size. Perhaps an approach towards evaluation that balances quantitative with qualitative data would be more appropriate for such a study. For example, observational reports by probation officers and teachers, subject interviews, self-assessment scales, monitoring incident reports, are all qualitative strategies that could be used. As a facilitator, one of the high points of conducting the sessions was observing the participants' reactions to the material, as well as their move towards cohesiveness as a group. This, of course, could not be measured quantitatively, but probably held a great deal of meaning relative to impacting valuational and belief structures.

It may also be helpful to add a control condition at each site that would also receive a non-Afro-centrically based intervention. Adding such a program or material could further distinguish the designed Afrocentric intervention from other types of anti-violence processes.

Greater emphasis and attention to structuring the pre- and post-testing process might also prove beneficial. Clear communication and planning between the researcher, the probation, and education components, and other significant components of the correctional facility as to the testing procedures, would provide structure and a level of safety for all involved. For example, during the orientation for this study, the researcher was faced with testing and managing the behavior of over fifty inmates with no staff present. Inmates, at some point, wandered off into the kitchen and stole food. Later it was found that these inmates were responsible for spitting in the soup, which caused problems for other inmates who attended the orientation session. This could have been avoided with clear communication and delegation of responsibilities.

In addition, simplifying the test-taking process would help to minimize future malingering. For example, the fifty-item Survey of Personal Beliefs could be reduced to ten items by pulling out the Frustration Tolerance Scale. The results could be augmented by comparing to other measures of frustration or indicators of frustration tolerance. Both the RADS and STAXI are relatively brief instruments and proved to offer more reliable results. Future research may also benefit by focusing on state anger (situational anger) and on anger suppression/expression as a more direct indicator of the intervention's short-term effect. Effect indicated by these scales would support evidence of the role of culturally relevant material in cognitive and interpersonal modalities.

Although the conceptualization of the client's problem areas may be different for cognitive therapies versus interpersonal therapies, there is often a high level of overlap. Cognitive and interpersonal therapies derive from a psychodynamic model, which may account for such overlap (Barnett, 1980). Both cognitive and interpersonal psychotherapy are often utilized in the treatment of depression, with cognitive therapy being similar to the analysis of defenses in the psychodynamic psychotherapies (Ursano & Hales, 1986). Revelation of defenses helps both patient and therapist focus on hidden cognitive distortions, which result in the patient's destructive perception of events. The same defense mechanisms utilized to minimize anxiety in dynamic therapy result in distortions of perception and cognition, which are the focus of cognitive psychotherapy. To the extent that culturally relevant and socio-historically based material aid in clarifying distortions of perception, inclusion of this material in mainstream therapies could certainly be effective.

In conclusion, qualitative findings suggest use of culturally relevant and socio-historically based information in the treatment of African-descended young men may impact factors antecedent to violent behavior. This has important implications for the practice of psychotherapy and for the development and utilization of Afrocentric models and methodology in the treatment of African-descended youth. African-American youth often do not have access to resources for long-term psychotherapy or other, much-needed, mental health services. Brief therapy and group therapy models become important cost-effective approaches for them. However, they need not be the only models considered to effect change in the targeted population. It is more important that Afrocentric methodology derived from Afrocentric theory and meta-theory (Myers, 2004) inform these approaches to psychological treatment if they are to be effective for African-American youth. The need to work in a community context becomes clear. As health is a social function as well as an individual one, movement from a lower to higher level of consciousness, according to Dr. Linda James Meyers (2013), is "for most people quite difficult, if not impossible to sustain, in a toxic, pathological social environment. Without clear culturally syntonic psychological insight and understanding, psycho-educational training and rebuilding of community and collective support and reinforcement, restoration of spirit is non-sustainable." Perhaps the above-described intervention could be utilized within the context of a communal health model such as Optimal Psychology, which addresses both psychic disarray as well as alignment and inoculation of the psyche for higher level functioning (Myers, 2003).

Given the indicated group movement along the stages of decomposition, germination, and transformation, further research in this area would be served by a detailed investigation of the path stages utilized (Nobles, 1986). Development of criteria for each stage could promote development of a framework for conceptualizing issues and challenges facing African-descended youth. Given the context of this study, developing and validating an instrument(s) designed to measure movement through and location within Nobles' stages could offer an important component in comparison to outcome variables.

Future study would be greatly advanced by utilizing assessments developed within the context of an African-centered framework (as none of the instruments used in this study had been). Use of instruments like the African Self-Consciousness Scale (ASCS) and the Cultural Misorientation Scale (CMS) in assessing ASC and CM is critical according to Kambon (2003; Kambon, Rackley 2005; Kambon and Bowen-Reid, 2010) to meaningfully evaluating African American behavior and mental health. These instruments have been used in various studies involving crucial variables such as personal causation, psychological well-being, health promoting behaviors and anti-Black behavior. Both instruments have been shown to be reliable and valid.

An additional area of emphasis for structuring programs with Afrocentric themes, as well as increasing the effectiveness of psychotherapeutic interventions, would be to discriminate between effects of exposure to information presented and issues of transference, as previously stated. In most rites of passage programs, clearly, youth are impacted cognitively by content presented and emotionally by the process, including the individual personalities involved in delivering the curriculum. These individuals or mentors often are charged with the responsibility of guiding participants through the program. Finally, developing criteria for the practical application of existing socio-psychological literature, with respect to its social etiology for mental health issues, would advance the development of Afrocentric treatment models. Advancing the utility of working within the framework of African Psychology can hold promise for effective treatment and prevention of disorders within the Black personality. This may include restoring the African Self-Conscious. This study endeavored to bridge the gap between psychological and sociological conceptualization of mental health related issues for young men of African descent. The applied nature of this research shows promise for psychological treatment of high-risk populations.

Appendix

MATERIALS

An important aspect of this study was the material utilized as treatment. The criteria for the material selected in the development of treatment protocol required that they (1) reflect Afrocentric thought and (2) reflect a "true" or an accurate representation of history according to Afrocentric historians. These materials were selected in order to impact the subjects' attitudes of perceived hopelessness and/or helplessness, and to motivate cultural/spiritual realignment.

The treatment modality, which aimed at impacting the structures (moral, intellectual, cultural, and valuational) stated above, incorporated a culturally appropriate format for teens with attention to maximum efficiency, considering time constraints. The methodology was designed to impact deeper psychological issues that underlie problem behavior and encounter the African-American male on his path of life development. It considered the path stages, introduced earlier, of decomposition, germination, transformation, and transcendence. The concept of path stages are espoused by author/sociologist Dr. Wade Nobles (1986) as a useful framework for guiding and utilizing Maatian principles. Assuming the existing decompositional status of African-American young men, the intervention was organized into three areas of decomposition, germination, and transformation.

INSTRUCTIONS FOR TWELVE-WEEK INTERVENTION

Decomposition Material

Decomposition material reflected the current status of socio-psychological racism, Black identity formation, and violence within the Black community, while offering a historical context. This material was presented to facilitate the expression of emotions relative to the socio-economic and psychosocial condition of Black males in America. Videotaped material was selected with this function in mind as well as for its utility in enhancing the joining process (i.e., considering the level of respect for, familiarity with, and influence of the speakers/artists on the study sample).

Session #1:

Lusane, G, *Pipe Dream Blues*. "Black youth, attacked, abandoned, angry and addicted" (pg. 22-24) (Discussion); "Racism and the drug crisis" (pg. 25-38) (hand out).

Farrakhan, L. (Speaker), Nation of Islam (Producer). *Stop The Killing* [Video] (2:14 - 4:15 / 43:00 - 58:00 min.).

Jackson, P. (Editor) News excerpts on Rodney King aftermath [Video] (1:20-1:46/2:08-2:24/2:47-6:38 min.).

Riggs, M. (Producer) *Ethnic Notions* [Video] (0-3:09/ 4:44-8:30/ 9:35-14:43/15:48-20:58).

Ice Cube (Vocals), Priority Records (1991, 1992). "Bird in the Hand"/ "Tear this _____ up" [CD Recording].

Instructions:

   a.) Play "Bird in the Hand" as introduction to segment.
   b.) Distribute and introduce the outline for *Pipe Dream Blues* and review for 10 minutes.
   c.) Have group view videotape of selection from *Ethnic Notions*.
   d.) Have group view videotape of news excerpts from Rodney King beating and L.A. rebellion.
   e.) Play "Tear this _____ up."
   f.) Have group view videotape of *Stop the Killing*.
   g.) Conduct brief discussion on information presented.

Session #2:

Riggs, M. (Producer) *Ethnic Notions* [Video] (22:06-25:48/40:14 - 47:42/ 54:07 - 55:05).

Hutchinson, E.O., *Crime, Drugs, and African-Americans: Legacy of Slavery/Quest for Power* (pp.3-5); *The Doping of the Ghetto* (pp. 8-10).

Prime Time Live (Producer). *True Colors* [Video] (Discussion).

Kush, I., *What They Never Told You in History Class* (pp. 1-13) (Handout).

Ice Cube (Vocals), Priority Records (1993). "I Wanna Kill Sam" [CD Recording].

Instructions:

  a.) Play "I Wanna Kill Sam."
  b.) Distribute copies of *Legacy of Slavery* and *The Doping of the Ghetto.* Read aloud and focus on underlined areas.
  c.) View *True Colors* videotape.
  d.) View *Ethnic Notions* videotape.
  e.) Distribute copies of *What They Never Told You in History Class*, review and discuss.

GERMINATION MATERIAL

Germination material offered new ideas regarding the origins of civilization and the historical contributions of African people, in an attempt to challenge some of the negative perceptions that may block the participants in realizing their potential. This material also focused on the concept of "collective being" as it relates to African-American young men.

Session #3:

Hilliard, A. & Middleton, L., Waset Educational Productions (Producer). *Free Your Mind, Return To The Source: African Origins* [Video] (00 - 16:40/ 16:40 - 41:00).

Wilson, A.N., "Black-on-Black Violence: The Psycho-Dynamics of Black Self-Annihilation" in *Service of White Domination: The Crucible of Identity* (pp. 29-31) (Discussion).

KRS-ONE (Vocals), Zomba Records (1989). "You Must Learn" [Audiotape Recording].

KRS-ONE (Vocals), Jive Records (1995). "The Truth" [Audiotape Recording].

Instructions:

a.) Listen to "You Must Learn" and "The Truth" audiotape. Briefly discuss.

b.) Distribute copies of *The Crucible of Identity* outline and discuss.

c.)View *Free Your Mind* videotape, segment #1 and briefly discuss.

d.) View *Free Your Mind* videotape, segment #2 and briefly discuss.

Session #4:

Karenga, M., Ivan Van Sertima (Producer). *African Contribution to World Science* [Audiotape Recording]. (12-30 min.)

Goody Mob (Vocals), La Face Records (1995). "Cell Therapy" on Soul Food [Audiotape Recording].

Free Your Mind, Return To The Source: African Origins Video: Dr. Asa Hilliard III and Listervelt Middleton. Producer: Waset Educational Productions. (41 - 55/ 56:40 -1:07.30/ 1:18.30 - 1:28 min.)

Instructions:

a.) Play "Cell Therapy." Briefly discuss.

b.) Play "African Contribution to World Science" audiotape. Briefly discuss.

c.) View *Free Your Mind* videotape. Discuss.

Session #5

Break The Chains Video. Producer: Big Joe Crash.

Free Your Mind, Return To The Source: African Origins Video: Dr. Asa Hilliard III and Listervelt Middleton. Producer: Waset Educational Productions. (1:28 - 1:41.32).

Metu Neter. Discussion on "Knowledge" (pg. 107); Author: Ra Un Nefer Amen.

Dr. Ivan Van Sertima: African Contribution to World Science, Audiotape. (30-60 min.)

Stolen Legacy. "Intro by Asa Hilliard"/ "Intro by George G.M. James"(pp.1-6); Author: George James.

Instructions:

a.) Distribute copies of "Knowledge". Review and discuss.

b.) View *Break the Chains* videotape.

c.) Listen to "African Contribution to World Science" audiotape. Discuss.

d.) Distribute and review "Stolen Legacy" Outline.

e.) View *Free Your Mind* videotape.

Session #6

Master Keys To Ancient Kemet Video: Dr. Asa Hilliard III and Listervelt Middleton. Producer: Waset Educational Productions. (02:00 - 22:00)

Blood. Goody Mob/ on Soul Food: La Face Records, 1995.

The Golden Age of The Moor. "The Moor: Light of Europe's Dark Age" (pg. 151-178), Author: Chandler / Editor: Van Sertima.

"God's Chosen People" Video: Rabbi J. Goldstein, Prof. Z. Garber, and Dr. Khallid Muhammed. (16-:23, 1:00-1:60, 1:78-2:38, 3:73-4:61, 7:16-7:98, 12:38-13:34, 13:98-15:68, 15:79-16:18, 19:70-20:27, 26:75-28:25, 30:87-38:31, 39:40-43:55)

Instructions:

    a.) Listen to "Blood".

    b.) View *Master Keys* videotape.

    c.) Distribute copies of "The Moor: Light of Europe's Dark Age" outline. Review and discuss.

    d.) View *God's Chosen People* videotape.

Session #7

God's Chosen People Video cont.: Rabbi J. Goldstein, Prof. Z. Garber, and Dr. Khallid Muhammed. (:16-:23, 1:00-1:60, 1:78-2:38, 3:73-4:61, 7:16-7:98, 12:38-13:34, 13:98-15:68, 15:79-16:18, 19:70-20:27, 26:75-28:25, 30:87-38:31, 39:40-43:55)

Afrikan Origins of Civilization I Video. (1:49-1:53 min.); Producer: Ashrwa Kwesi. (Capstone and symbols on dollar bills)

Afrikan Origins of Civilization II Video. (:2-:10 min. Neophyte, Obelisk. - :10:30-:26, Destruction of images, Kemetian historical figures, - :48-1:00, Images of our ancestors, Museum) Producer: Ashrwa Kwesi

"One million niggaz inside." Goody Mob on Soul Food: La Face Records, 1995.

Instructions:

    a.) View *God's Chosen people* videotape.

    b.) Listen to "One million niggaz inside".

    c.) View *Afrikan Origins of Civilization* videotape.

TRANSFORMATION MATERIAL

Transformation material focused on questions relative to the participants: What is their path? At what stage do they presently exist? And how do their perceptions create reality? This material attempted to challenge participants' culturally distorted ideas about themselves and to culturally realign their behavior with Afrocentric principles of conduct.

Session #8

"*God's Chosen People Pt. 2*" Video: Rabbi J. Goldstein, Prof. Z. Garber, Dr. Khallid Muhammed. (44-74 min.)
   The Clegg Series: Egypt During the Golden Age Video. (3-29 min.); Producer: Legrand Clegg.
   Young Players Gonna Get It Together Video. Producer: Priority Records.

Instructions:

   a.) View *God's Chosen People* video.
   b.) View *Egypt During the Golden Age* videotape.
   c.) View *Young Players Gonna Get It Together* videotape. Discuss.

Session #9

African Origins of Judeo Christianity video: Ashrwa Kwesi (1-10 min.)
   Keynote Address: 1986 Conference of The Association of Black Psychologists Audiotape: Dr. Ivan Van Sertima (10-43 min.)
   Save The Family Video: Min. Farrakhan (30-45 min.)

Instructions:

   a.) View videotape.
   b.) Listen to *Keynote Address* audiotape.
   c.) View segment of *Save the Family* videotape. Discuss.

Session #10

Runoko Rashidi Video: African Contributions To The World (5-1:20 min.)
   Instructions:
   a.) View *African Contributions to The World* videotape. Discuss.
   Session #11
   1986 Conference of The Association of Black Psychologists Audiotape: Panel Discussion: Dr. Naim Akbar (5- 15 min.)
   Dr. Welsing: Cress Theory of Color Confrontation and Racism (pp. 1-10) discussion.
   African Origins of Judeo Christianity video: Ashrwa Kwesi (1-10 min.)

Instructions:

a.) Listen to *Nile Valley Conference* audiotape. Discuss.

b.) Distribute copies of *Cress Theory* outline. Review and discuss.

c.) View *African Origins of Judeo Christianity* videotape.

Session #12

Master Keys To Ancient Kemet Video: Dr. Asa Hilliard III and Listervelt Middleton. Producer: Waset Educational Productions. (13-35, 40- 1:05:00 min.)

American Society/Crimogenic Society: *Amos Wilson* (pp. 35-45)

Instructions:

a.) Distribute copies of *Crimogenic Society* outline. Review and discuss.

b.) View "Master Keys" videotape. Discuss.

References

Abraham, W. E. (1962), The Mind of Africa. University of Chicago Press; Chicago, IL.

Abrams, D. S. Bertrand, M. & Mullainathan, S. (June, 2012), *Do Judges Vary in Their Treatment of Race?* Institute for Law & Economic Research. Paper No. 11-07; Journal of Legal Studies, 41 (2), pp. 347-383, University of Pennsylvania.

ACLU report (June 6, 2008). Locating the School to Prison Pipeline.

Akbar, N. (1980). Homicide among Black males: Causal factors. Public Health Report, 95, 549.

Akbar, N. (1985). Chains and images of psychological slavery. Jersey City, NJ: New Mind Productions.

Akbar, N. (1986). Special panel presentation, Africa/world civilization: Historical and psychological perspectives [Audiotape recording]. Association of Black Psychologists Conference, Oakland, CA.

Akbar, N. (1996), *Breaking the chains of Psychological Slavery*. Mind Productions and Associates, Tallahassee, FL.

Akbar, N., (1996). African Metapsychology of Human Personality. In Azibo (Ed.), *African Psychology in Historical Perspective and Related Commentary*. Africa World Press: Trenton, NJ.

Akbar, N., (2003). *Mental Disorders of African Americans* in Akbar Papers in African Psychology (pp. 160–177).

Als, H.; Lewis, J. and Litwack, L. F. (2000). Without Sanctuary: Essays, (Ed.) Allen, J.; Twin Palms Publishers/Twelvetrees Press. Santa Fe, New Mexico.

Amen, R. (1990). Metu Neter: The great oracle of Tehuti and the Egyptian system of spiritual cultivation. Bronx: Khamit Corp.

Amsel, A. (1958). The role of frustrative nonreward in noncontinuous reward situations. Psychological Bulletin, 55,102-119.

Amsel, A. (1992). Frustration theory: An analysis of dispositional learning and memory. New York: Cambridge University Press.

Averill, J. R. (1980). A constructive view of emotions. In R. Pluthik, & H. Kellerman (Eds.), Theories of emotions. New York: Academic.

Averill J. (1982). Anger and aggression: An essay on emotion. In F. Kidd (Ed.), Springer Series in Social Psychology. New York: Springer-Verlag.

Ax, A. F. (1953). Physiological differentiation of emotional states. Psychosomatic Medicine, 15, 433-422.

Azibo, D. A., (1991). Towards a metatheory of the African personality. The Journal of Black Psychology, 17(2), 37-45.

Azibo, D.A., (1996). Mental Health Defined Afrocentrically. In Azibo (Ed.), African Psychology in Historical Perspective and Related Commentary. Africa World Press: Trenton, NJ.

Baggio, M. K. (1987). Clinical dimensions of anger management. American Journal of Psychotherapy, 41(3), 417-427.

Baldwin, J. A. (1981). Notes on an Afrocentric theory of Black personality testing. Western Journal of Black Studies, 5(3), 170-179.

Barham, J. (1992). Has violent crime really increased? A comparison of violence rates reported by the two U.S. Department of Justice data sets. A paper presented to the American Psychological Association Commission on Youth and Violence, based on testimony to the U.S. General Accounting Office, April 19, 1990.

Barker, R., Dembo, T., & Lewin, K. (1941). Frustration and regression: An experiment with young children. University of Iowa study in child welfare, Whole #386.

Barnett, J. (1980). Interpersonal processes, cognition and the analysis of character. Contemporary Psychoanalysis, 39, 291-301.

Beck, A. T. (1973). The diagnosis and management of depression. Philadelphia: University of Pennsylvania Press.

Beck, A. T. (1976). Cognitive therapy and emotional disorders. New York: International Universities Press.

Berkowitz, L. (1962). Aggression: A social psychological analysis. New York: McGraw-Hill.

Binder, J., Henry, W., & Strupp, H. (1987). An appraisal of selection criteria for dynamic psychotherapies and implications for setting time limits. Psychiatry, 50, 154-166.

Biskin, B. (1988). Review of the State-Trait Anger Expression Inventory, Research Edition. In J. J. Kramer, & J. C. Conoley (Eds.), Mental Measurements Yearbook. Buros Institute of Mental Measurements: Univ. of Nebraska Press.

Bohart, A. C. (1980). Toward a cognitive theory of catharsis. Psychotherapy: Theory, Res. Pract., 17, 192-201.

Braxton, E. T. (1992). A new intervention paradigm. In M. R. Issacs (Ed.), Violence: The impact of community violence on African-American children and families. Arlington, VA: National Center for Education in Maternal and Child Health.

CNN News Report on Correctional Association of New York Statistics. September 8, 2012.

Brown, J. S., & Farber, I. E. (1951). Emotions conceptualized as intervening variables-with suggestions toward a theory of frustration. Psychological Bulletin, 48, 465-495.

Buck, R. (1980). Non-verbal behavior and the theory of emotion: The facial feedback hypothesis. Journal of Personality and Social Psychology, 38, 810-824.

Buck, R. (1983). Emotional development and emotional education. In R. Plutchik & H. Kellerman (Eds.), Emotion: Theory, research, and experience. New York: Academic Press.

Canson, P. E. (1993). The Federal Violence Initiative: A Question of Ethical Procedure. Paper. CSPP; Alameda, CA.

Corrado, R. and A. Peters (2013). Community-based intervention programs for released incarcerated serious and violent young offenders: Challenges and opportunities. In Risk Assessment for Juvenile Violent Offending; Baldry and Kapardis, Eds. Routledge, NY, NY.

Carruthers, J. H. (1990). Divine Speech: The foundation of Kemetic wisdom. In M. Karenga (Ed.), Reconstructing Kemetic culture: Papers, perspectives, projects (pp. 3-23). Los Angeles: University of Sankore Press.

Centers for Disease Control. (1990). Homicide among young Black males-United States, 1978-1987. Morbidity and Mortality Weekly Report, 39, 869-873.

Child, I. L., & Waterhouse, I. K. (1952). Frustration and the quality of performance: I. A critique of the Barker, Dembo and Lewin experiment. Psychology Review, 59, 351-362.

Clark, C. (1990). Emotions and micropolitics in everyday life: Some patterns and paradoxes of "place." In T. D. Kemper (Ed.), Research agendas in the sociology of emotions. New York: State University of New York Press.

Comer, J. P. (1969). White Racism: Its Root, Form, and Function Am J Psychiatry;126:802-806. American Psychological Association.

Cross, T., Bazron, B., Dennis, K., & Issacs, M. (1989). Towards a culturally competent system of care. Washington, DC: CASSP Technical Assistance Center.

Cunningham, R. T. & Mizelle, R. (1993). The effects of "African-American Manhood Training" (A rite of passage model) on the self-concept of African-American adolescent males. Psych Discourse, 24(6), 8-11.

Cress-Welsing, F. (1991). *The Cress Theory of Color-Confrontation and Racism (White Supremacy): A Psychogenetic Theory and World Outlook* in The Isis Papers: Third World Press; Chicago, IL.

Davies, J. (1989). Letter to the editor. Political Psychology, 10(1), 177-181.

Davidson, J. (October, 1997). *Crime Pays. Cashing in on Black Prisoners, Caged Cargo.* Emerge Magazine.

Data Snapshot: Kids Count (February, 2013). Reducing Youth Incarceration in the United States. The Annie E. Casey Foundation. www.aecf.org.

Demaria, T., Kassinove, H., & Dill, C. (1989). Psychometric properties of the Survey of Personal Beliefs: A rational-emotive measure of irrational thinking. Journal of Personality Assessment, 53(2), 329-341.

DeGruy, Leary, J. (2005). Post Traumatic Slave Syndrome: America's Legacy of Enduring Injury and Healing (pp.114-182, 54, 73). Milwaukie, Oregon: Uptone Press.

Diop, C. A. (1974) The African origin of civilization. New York: Lawrence Hill.

Diop, C. A. (1978.) The Cultural Unity of Black Africa. Third World Press: Chicago, IL.

Diop, C. A. (1991). Civilization or barbarism: An authentic anthropology. New York: Lawrence Hill.

Dollard, J., Doob, L., Miller, N., Mowrer, O., & Sears, R. (1939). Frustration and aggression. New Haven, CT: Yale University Press.

Durel, L. A., & Krantz, D. S. (1985). The possible effects of beta-adrenergic blocking drugs on behavioral and psychological concomitants of anger. In M. A. Chesney & R. H. Rosenman (Eds.), Anger and hostility in cardiovascular and behavioral disorders. Washington, DC: Hemisphere.

Dyson, J. L. (1990). The effect of family violence on children's academic performance and behavior. Journal of the National Medical Association, 82, 17-22.

Eberhardt, J. L.; Goff, P. A.; Purdie, V. J.; Davies, P. G. (2004).

Seeing Black: Race, Crime, and Visual Processing, *Journal of Personality and Social Psychology*, Vol. 87(6), 876-893.

Eckman, P., Friesen, W. V., & Ellsworth, P. (1972). Emotion in the human face. New York: Permagon.

Elliot, D., Huizinga, D., & Morse, B. (1986). Self-reported violent offending: A descriptive analysis of juvenile violent offenders and their offending careers. Journal of Interpersonal Violence, 1, 472-513.

Ellis, A. (1962). Reason and Emotion in Psychotherapy. New York: Lyle Stuart.

Endicott, J., & Spitzer, R. L. (1978). A diagnostic interview: The schedule for affective disorders and schizophrenia. Archives of General Psychiatry, 35, 837-844.

Entringer,S.; Epel, E. S.; Lin, J.; Buss, C.; Blackburn, E. H.; Simhan, H. N.; Wadhwa, P. D.; Prenatal Programming of Infant Telomere Length. European Journal of Psychotraumatology Supplement 1, 2012-3 http://dx.doi.org/10.3402/ejpt.v3i0.19477

Erickson, E. (1968). Identity, youth and crisis. New York: W. W. Norton.

Farrington, K., (1986). The application of stress theory to the study of family violence: Principles, problems, and prospects. Journal of Family Violence, 1(2), 131-147.

Fingerhut, L., Ingram, D., & Feldman, J. (1992). Firearm and nonfirearm homicide among persons 15 through 19 years of age. Journal of the American Medical Association, 267, 3048-3053.

Fitzpatrick, K. M.; Boldizar, J. P. (1993). The prevalence and consequences of exposure to violence among African-American youth. Journal of the American Academy of Child Adolescent Psychiatry, 32(2), 424-430.

Fu-Kia, K. K. B.; Self-Healing Power and Therapy: Old Teachings from Africa. Black Classic Press; Inprint Editions: Baltimore, MD; 2003.

Gibbs, J. T. (1988). Health and mental health of young Black males. In J. T. Gibbs (Ed.), Young Black and male in America: An endangered species (pp. 219-243). Westport, CT: Auburn House.

Gilbert, P. (1992). Depression: The evolution of powerlessness. New York: The Guilford Press.

Glueck, S., & Glueck, E. (1950). Unraveling juvenile delinquency. Cambridge, MA: Harvard University Press.

Goff, P. A., Jackson, M. C., Di Leone, B. A. L., Culotta, C. M., & DiTomasso, N. A. (2014, February 24). The Essence of Innocence: Consequences of Dehumanizing Black Children. *Journal of Personality and Social Psychology*: Advance online publication. http://dx.doi.org/10.1037/a0035663

Gordon, M., (1992). Theoretical and conceptual frameworks. In M. R. Issacs (Ed.), Violence: The impact of community violence on African-American children and families. Arlington, VA: National Center for Education in Maternal and Child Health.

Gopnik, Adam (January 2012). "The Caging of America: Why do we lock up so many people?", The New Yorker Magazine.

Graham, S., & Hudley, C. (1992). An attributional approach to aggression in African-American children. In D. Schunk, & J. Meece (Eds.), Student perceptions in the classroom (pp. 75-94). Hillsdale, NJ.: Earlbaum.

Greenwood, P. (1992). Reforming California's approach to delinquent and high-risk youth. In J. B. Steinberg, D. W. Lyon, & M. E. Vaiana (Eds.), Urban America: Policy choices for Los Angeles and the nation. Santa Monica, CA: Rand.

Grier, W. H. & Cobbs, P. M. (1968). Black Rage. Basic Books Inc.; New York, NY.

Guerra, N., & Slaby, R. (1990). Cognitive mediators of aggression in adolescent offenders: 2 intervention. *Developmental Psychology*, 26, 269-277.

Guthrie, R. V. (1976). Even the rat was White. New York: Harper and Row.

Guthrie, R. V. (1998). Even the rat was White. (2nd Ed.) Needham Heights, MA: Allyn and Bacon.

Hakeem, M. (1957-1958). A critique of the psychiatric approach to the prevention of juvenile delinquency. Social Problems, 5, 194-205.

Hammond, R. W. (1990). Dealing with anger: Givin' it, takin' it, workin' it out. Champaign, IL: Research Press.

Hammond, R. W. & Yung, B. (1993). Psychology's role in the public health response to assaultive violence among young African-American men. American Psychologist, 48(2), 142-154.

Hardiman, J. W. (1990). The ancient Egyptian perceptual frame of reference. In M. Karenga (Ed.), Reconstructing Kemetic culture: Papers, perspectives, projects (pp. 136-141). Los Angeles, CA: University of Sankore Press.

Harvey, A. R. (1989). Extended family: A universal and naturalistic salvation for African Americans. Proceedings of the Black Agenda: Building on our strengths: A celebration of the African American family conference. Washington, DC: Black Task Force on Child Abuse and Neglect.

Harvey, A. R. (1992). Violence: A reaction to racial and cultural oppression. In M. R. Issacs (Ed.) Violence: The impact of community violence on African-American children and families. Arlington, VA: National Center for Education in Maternal and Child Health.

Hawkins, D. (1986). Longitudinal-situational approaches to understanding Black-on-Black homicide. In Report of the Secretary's task force on Black and minority health (Vol. 5, pp. 97-116). Washington, DC: U.S. Department of Health and Human Services.

Henry, J. P., & Stephens, P. M. (1977). Stress, health and the social environment: A sociobiologic approach to medicine. New York: Springer Verlag.

Hill, H. (1992). Social and emotional development. In M. R. Issacs (Ed.), Violence: The impact of community violence on African-American children and families. Arlington, VA: National Center for Education in Maternal and Child Health.

Hilliard, Asa G.; *Free Your Mind, Return to the Source: The African Origin of Civilization*. San Francisco: Urban Institute for Human Services, 1978.

Hilliard, A. G. III, (1991). Introduction. In A. G. Hilliard (Ed.), Testing African American students (pp. 40-44). Morristown, NJ: Aaron Press.

Hilliard, A. (1995). *The Maroon Within Us*: Black Classic Press; Baltimore, MD.

Hilliard, A. and Middleton, L. (1991). Free Your Mind, Return To the Source: African Origins of Civilization. Waset Educational Productions; San Francisco, CA.

Hirschi, T., and Kelvin, H. C. (1967). Delinquency research: An appraisal of analytic methods. New York: Free Press.

Hohmann, G. (1966). Some effects of spinal cord lesions on experiential emotional feelings. *Psychophysiology*, 3, 143-156.

Hovland, C., & Sears, R. R. (1940). Minor studies of aggression VI. Correlation of lynchings with economic indices. *Journal of Psychology. Interdisciplinary and Applied*, 9, 301-310.

Hutchinson, E. O. (1990). Crime, drugs and African-Americans. Inglewood, CA: Impact Publications.

Issacs, M. R. (1992). Violence: The impact of community violence on African-American children and families. Arlington, VA: National Center for Education in Maternal and Child Health.

Jackson, T. P. (2012); Race, Politics and the Case for why White America Could Elect a Sociopath over the Black Man: Lessons from the "Real McCoy." *Gibbsmagazine.com* http://www.gibbsmagazine.com/Race%20politics%20and%20real%20McCoy.htm

Jackson, T. P. & Ettinger, R. H. (2013), *Psychology: Connections in Theory and Practice (4ᵗʰ ed.)*. BVT Publishing; Redding, CA.

James, G. M. (1985). Stolen legacy. San Francisco, CA: Julian Richardson Associates.

James, W. (1884). What is an emotion? Mind, 9, 188-205.

James, W. (1893). Psychology. New York: Holt.

Jones, F. (2007). What Have We Done To Our Children–Positioning Black Children for Success: Gibbs-Mirror Publication; Oakland, CA.

Juvenile Justice Outcome Evaluation Report (2010). *Youth Released from the Division of Juvenile Justice in Fiscal Year 2004-05*. California Department of Corrections and Rehabilitation; Sacramento, CA.

Kambon, K. K. K. (1992). The African personality in America: An African-centered framework. Tallahassee, FL: Nubian Nation Publications.

Kambon, K. K. K. (1998). African/Black Psychology in the American Context: An African-Centered Approach. Tallahassee, FL: Nubian Nation Publications

Kambon, K. K. K. (2003). Cultural Misorientation: The Greatest Threat to the Survival of the Black Race in the 21ˢᵗ Century. Tallahassee, FL: Nubian Nation Publications.

Kambon, K. & Rackley, R. (2005). The Cultural Misorientation Scale/CMS: Psychometric assessment. *Journal of Africana Studies Research*, I(1), 15-34.

Kambon, K. K. K. (2006). Chapter Three: The Psychology of Oppression; In Kambon's Reader in Liberation Psychology. Tallahassee, FL: Nubian Nation Publications. Selected Works, Vol.1, pp. 55-72.

Kambon, K. K. K. (2006). Chapter Five: African Self-consciousness and the Mental Health of African Americans; In Kambon's Reader in Liberation Psychology. Tallahassee, FL: Nubian Nation Publications. Selected Works, Vol.1, pp. 92-106.

Kambon, K.; Bowen-Reid, T. (2010). Theories of African American Personality: Classification, Basic Constructs and Empirical Predictions/Assessment. *The Journal of Pan African Studies*, Vol. 3 (8) pp. 83-108.

Kaplan, B., Kundert, D. (1988). Review of the Reynolds Adolescent Depression Scale. In J. J. Kramer, & J. C. Conoley (Eds.), Mental Measurements Yearbook. Buros Institute of Mental Measurements. Lincoln, NB: Univ. of Nebraska Press.

Karenga, M. (1990). Towards a sociology of Maatian ethics: Literature and context. In M. Karenga (Ed.) Reconstructing Kemetic culture: Papers, perspectives, projects (pp. 66-96). Los Angeles, CA: University of Sankore Press.

Kazdin, A. (1987). Treatment of anti-social behavior in children: Current status and future directions. Psychological Bulletin, 102, 187-203.

Kellerman, H. (1979). Group psychotherapy and personality: Intersecting structures. New York: Grune and Stratton.

Kharrazian, D. (2013); Why isn't my Brain working?: A Revolutionary understanding of brain decline and effective strategies to recover your brain's health. Elephant Press. Carlsbad, CA.

King, R., (1990). African origin of biological psychiatry, Germantown: Seymour and Smith.

Kunjufu, J. (2004). Solutions For Black America. African American Images: Chicago, IL.

Laird, J. D. (1974). Self-attribution of emotion: The effects of expressive behavior on the quality of emotional experience. Journal of Personality and Social Psychology, 29, 475-486.

Langan, P. (1991). Rate of growth in U.S. prison system? Bureau of Justice Statistics

Langan, P., & Graziadei, H. (1992). Felony sentencing in state courts. Bureau of Justice statistics report.

Lawson, R. (1965). Frustration: The development of a scientific concept, Critical issues in psychology series. New York: Macmillan Company.

Lee, B., Carter, H. L., Cooley, D. L., & King, G. D. (1992). Opportunity or chaos: A generation in peril (preliminary report). Sacramento, CA: The California Commission on the Status of African-American Males.

Lee, C. (1987). Black manhood training: Group counseling for male Blacks in grades 7-12. Journal for Specialists in Group Work, 12 (1), 18-25.

Leventhal, H., & Mosbach, P. (1983). The perceptual-motor theory of emotion. In J. Cacioppo, & R. Petty (Eds.), Social Psychophysiology. New York: Guilford Press.

Leventhal, H. (1980). Toward a comprehensive theory of emotion. In L. Berkowitz (Ed.), Advances in experimental social psychology (Vol. 13). New York: Academic.

Loeber, R., & Dishion, T. (1983). Early predictors of male delinquency: A review. Psychological Bulletin, 94(1), 68-99.

Lusane, C. (1991). Pipe dream blues: Racism and the war on drugs. Boston, MA: South End Press.

Maier, N. R. F. (1949). Frustration. New York: McGraw-Hill.

Maier, N. R. F. (1956). The integrative value of concepts in frustration theory. Journal of Counseling Psychology, 23, 195-206.

May, J. M. (1986). Cognitive processes and violent behavior in young people. Journal of Adolescence, 9, 17-27.

MEE Report, The (1992). Reaching the hip hop generation. Philadelphia: MEE Productions/ Robert Wood Johnson Foundation.

Mendel, R.; (2011); *No Place for Kids:The Case for Reducing Juvenile Incarceration.* The Annie E. Casey Foundation; Baltimore, MD.

Messner, S., & Sampson, R. (1991). The sex ratio, family disruption, and rates of violent crime: The paradox of demographic structure. Social Forces, 69, 693-713.

Mills, R. C., Dunham, R. G., & Alpert G. P. (1988). Working with high-risk youth in prevention and early intervention programs: Toward a comprehensive wellness model. Adolescence, 23(91), 643-660.

Misplaced Priorities: Over Incarcerate, Under Educate; Excessive Spending on Incarceration Undermines Educational Opportunity and Public Safety in Communities. NAACP; April, 2011.

Monahan, J. (1989). The prediction of violent behavior: Toward a second generation of theory and policy. American Journal of Psychiatry, 141(1), pp. 10-15.

Muran, J. C., Kassinove, H.; Ross, S., & Muran, E. (1989). Irrational thinking and negative emotionality in college students and applicants for mental health services. Journal of Clinical Psychology, 45(2), 188-193.

Myers, L. J. (1988). Understanding an Afrocentric world view: Introduction to an optimal psychology. Dubuque, IA: Kendall/Hunt.

Myers, L.J. (2004). *Blessed assurance: Deep thought and meditations in the tradition of wisdom from our ancestors.* Gahanna, OH: The institute for Optimal Transformation and Leadership.

Myers, L.J. (2003). *Our health matters: Guide to an African (Indigenous) American psychology and cultural model for creating a climate and culture of optimal; health.* Columbus: Ohio Commission on Minority Health

Myers, L.J. (2013). *Restoration of Spirit: An African-Centered Communal Health Model. Journal of Black Psychology,* 39(3) 257-260.

NAACP Legal Defense and Educational Fund, Inc.; Ending the School-to-Prison Pipeline; Hearing: United States Senate Committee on the Judiciary Subcommittee on the Constitution, Civil Rights, and Human Rights (December 10, 2012), Damon T. Hewitt, Director,

Education Practice Group, Eric Rafael González, Education Policy Advocate, Education Practice Group.

National Center for Health Statistics (1992). Unpublished data tables from the NCHS Mortality Tapes, FBI-SHR. Atlanta, GA: Centers for Disease Control.

Nelson, G. (2011). "The Plot Against Hip Hop", Akashic Books: New York, NY.

Nobles, W. (1986). Africa/world civilization: Historical and psychological perspectives. Special panel presented at Association of Black Psychologists Conference, Oakland, CA.

Nobles, W. (1989). The Hawk Federation and the development of Black adolescent males: Toward a solution to the crises of America's young Black men. (Testimony before the Select Committee on Children, Youth, and Families, Congressional Hearings on America's Young Black Men: Isolated and in Trouble, July 25, 1989.)

Nobles, W. (1991). Psychometrics and African-American reality: A question of cultural antimony. In A. G. Hilliard (Ed.), Testing African-American students (pp. 45-55). Morristown, NJ: Aaron Press.

Nobles, W. W., Goddard, L. L., Cavil, W. E., & George, P. Y. (1987). The culture of drugs in the Black community. In W. W. Nobles (Ed.), Executive summary of a clear and present danger and the climate of drugs and service delivery. Oakland, CA: Black Family Institute.

Nobles, W.W. (2007). Shattered consciousness and fractured identity: The lingering psychological effects of the transatlantic slave trade experience. In Illinois Trans-Atlantic Slave Trade Commission Report I. Chicago: Jacob H. Carruthers Center of Inner City Studies, Northeastern Illinois University.

Nobles, W.W. (2013). *Natural/Man-Made Disaster and the Derailment of the African Worldview*. Journal of Black Psychology; 39(3) 252-256.

Novaco, R. W. (1979). The cognitive regulation of anger and stress. In P.C. Kendall, & S. D. Hollon (Eds.), Cognitive-behavioral interventions: Theory, research, procedures. New York: Academic.

O'Donnell, L., Cohen, D., & Hausman, A. (1991). Evaluation of community-based violence prevention programs. Public Health Reports, 106, 276-277.

Ogbu, J. U. (1987). Variability in minority responses to schooling: Nonimmigrants vs. immigrants. In G. Spindler, & L. Spindler (Eds.), Interpretive ethnography of education: At home and abroad (pp. 255-280). Hillsdale, NJ: Lawrence Earlbaum Assoc.

Oliver, W. (1989). Black males and social problems: Prevention through Afrocentric socialization. Journal of Black Studies, 20(1), 15-39.

One in 31: The Long Reach of American Corrections (March, 2009). The PEW Center On The States.

Osofsky, J. Chronic community violence: What is happening to our children. Psychiatry.

Parham, T.; White, J.; Ajamu, A. (2000). *African-Centered Psychology in the Modern Era*. In The Psychology of Blacks (3rd Ed.): Prentice Hall; Upper Saddle River, NJ.

Parham, T. A., Ajamu, A., White, J. L. (2011); *The Spiritual Core of African-Centered Psychology* (pp 35-49). The Psychology of Blacks: Centering Our Perspectives in the African Consciousness, 4ed., Prentice Hall, Boston, MA.

PBS Tavis Smiley Reports, Amurao, C. (2013). Fact Sheet: *How Bad Is the School-to-Prison Pipeline?* Episode 6: Education Under Arrest.

Petersilia, J. (1992). Crime and punishment in California: Full cells, empty pockets, and questionable benefits. In J. B. Steinberg, D. W. Lyon, & M. E. Vaiana (Eds.), Urban America: Policy choices for Los Angeles and the nation. Santa Monica, CA: Rand.

Pierce, C. M. (1970). Offense mechanisms. In Barbour (Ed.), The Black 70's. Boston: Porter Sargent Publications.

Pontoretto, J., & Benesch, K. (1988). An organizational framework for understanding the role of culture counseling. Journal of Counseling and Development, 66, 237-241.

Popplestone, J. A. & Mcpherson, M. W.(Eds.) (1988). Dictionary of Concepts in General Psychology. New York: Greenwood Press.

Postcards From The Edge (2004). http://withoutsanctuary.org.

Pouissaint, A. (1972). Why Blacks kill Blacks. New York: Emerson Hall.

Price, J. S. (1989). The effects of social stress on the behaviour and physiology of monkeys. In K. Davison and A. Kerr (Eds.), Contemporary themes in psychiatry. London: Gaskell: Royal College of Psychiatrists.

Price, J. S., & Sloman, L. (1987). Depression as yielding behavior: An animal model based on Schjelderup-Ebbe's pecking order. Ethology and Sociobiology, 8, 85-98.

Progressive Life Center Annual Report (2009). Transformation. Washington, D.C.

Pynoos, R. S. & Nader, K. (1987). Psychological first aid and treatment approach to children exposed to community violence: Research implications. Journal of Traumatic Stress. 1(4), 445-471.

Reynolds, W. M., & Coats, K. I. (1986). A comparison of cognitive-behavioral therapy and relaxation training for the treatment of depression in adolescents. Journal of Consulting and Clinical Psychology, 54, 653-660.

Rhodes, J., & Jason, L. (1988). Preventing substance abuse among children and adolescents. New York: Pergamon Press.

Richters, J., & Martinez, P. (1993). The NIMH Community Violence Project: 1. Children as victims and witness to violence, and 2. Children's distress symptoms associated with violence exposure. Psychiatry 56(1), 7-21.

Richardson, J. and Robillard, A. (2013); The Least of These: Chronic Exposure to Violence and HIV Risk Behaviors Among African American Male Violent Youth Offenders Detained in an Adult Jail; Journal of Black Psychology, 39(1) 28-62.

Ridley, C. (1985). Imperatives for ethnic and cultural relevance in psychology training programs. Professional Psychology: Research and Practice, 16, 611-622.

Roberts, R., (1990). Metu Neter: A matrix for the study of ancient Kemet. In M. Karenga (Ed.), Reconstructing Kemetic culture: Papers, perspectives, projects. Los Angeles, CA: University of Sankore Press.

Robinson, R. (2001), The Debt: What America Owes to Blacks. Plume/Penguin Group. New York, NY.

Rokaw, W., Mercy, J., & Smith, J. (1990). Comparing death certificate data with FBI crime reporting statistics on U.S. homicides. Public Health Reports; 105, 447-455.

Roman, J. (July, 2013); Race, Justifiable Homicide, and Stand Your Ground Laws: An Analysis of FBI Supplementary Homicide Report Data. Urban Institute.

Roman, J. Is American Criminal Justice Color Blind? The Statistics Say No. http://blog. metrotrends.org/2013/07/american-criminal-justice-color-blind-statistics. July 16, 2013.

Rosenberg, M., & Simmons, R. (1971). Black and White self-esteem: The urban school child. Washington, DC: American Sociological Association.

Rosenzweig, S. (1934). Types of reaction to frustration: An heruristic classification. Journal Abnormal Social Psychology, 29, 298-300.

Rosenzweig, S. (1939). The experimental study of regression. In H. A. Murray (Ed.), Explorations in Personality. New York: Oxford.

Rosenzweig, S. (1945). Further comparative data on repetition-choice after success and failure, as related to frustration-tolerance. Journal of Genetic Psychology, 66, 75-81.

Russell, B. (1961). An outline of philosophy. Cleveland, OH: World.

Sapolsky, R. M. (1989). Hypercortisolism among socially subordinate wild baboons originates at the CNS level. Archives of General Psychiatry, 46, 1047-1051.

Schachter, S. (1964). The interaction of cognitive and physiological determinants of emotional state. In Berkowitz (Ed.), Advances in experimental social psychology (Vol. 1). New York: Academic.

Shakoor, B. H., & Chalmers, D. (1990). Co-victimization of African-American children who witness violence: Effects on cognitive, emotional, and behavioral development. Journal of the National Medical Association, 83(3), 233-238.

Shalev, I.; Moffitt, T. E.; Caspi, A.; Childhood Trauma and Telomere Maintenance: European Journal of Psychotraumatology Supplement 1, 2012-3 http://dx.doi.org/10.3402/ejpt.v3i0.19505

Sheldon, R. G.; Teji, S. (July, 2012); *Collateral Consequences of Interstate Transfer of Prisoners*: Center On Juvenile and Criminal Justice. San Francisco, CA.

Skogan, W. G.; Hartnett, S. M.; Bump, N., and Dubois, J. (2008). Evaluation of CeaseFire-Chicago. Chicago, IL: Northwestern University.

Slaby, R., & Guerra, N. (1988). Cognitive mediators of aggression in adolescent offenders: I. Assessment. Developmental Psychology, 24, 580-588.

Spielberger, C. D., Johnson, E. H., Russel, S. F., Crane, R. J., Jacobs, G. A., & Worden, T. J. (1985). The experience and expression of anger: Construction and validation of an anger expression scale. In M. A. Chesney, & R. H. Rosenman (Eds.), Anger and hostility in cardiovascular and behavioral disorders. Washington, DC: Hemisphere.

Spielberger, C. D., Jacobs, G. A., Russel, S., F. & Crane, R. S. (1983). Assessment of anger: the state-trait anger scale. In J. Butcher, & C. D. Spielberger (Eds.), Advances in personality assessment (Vol. 2). Hillside, NJ: Earlbaum.

Spivak, H., Hausman, A. J., & Prothrow-Stith, D. (1989). Practitioner's forum: Public health and the primary prevention of adolescent violence- The violence prevention project. Violence and Victims, Vol. 4(3), 203-212.

Stampp, K. (1956). The peculiar institution: Slavery in the ante-bellum South, New York: Vintage Books.

Stark, E. (1990, July 18). The myth of black violence. New York Times, p. A21.

Stop and Frisk: The Human Impact; The Stories Behind The Numbers/The Effects On Our Communities (2012). Center for Constitutional Rights Report. New York, NY.

Storr, A. (1968). Human aggression. New York: Atheneum.

Terry, R. (1996). Kawanza: The seven principles. New York: Peter Pauper Press.

Tucker, C.; "Black jail rate cause for worry," San Francisco Chronicle; 2003. Misplaced priorities (NAACP report) 2011.

Turner, B. S. (1987). Medical power and social knowledge. London: Sage.

Ursano, R. & Hales, R (1986). A review of brief individual psychotherapies. American Journal of Psychiatry, 143(12), 1507-1517.

Van Sertima, I. (1992); Golden Age of the Moors: Journal of African Civilizations: Transaction Publishers.

Williams, C. (1976). The destruction of Black civilization: Great issues of a race from 4500 B.C. to 2000 A.D. Chicago: Third World Press.

Wilson, A. (1990). Black-on-Black Violence: The Psychodynamics of Black self-annihilation in service of White domination. New York: African World Infosystems Press.

Wilson, A. (1993). The falsification of Afrikan consciousness: Eurocentric history psychiatry and the politics of White supremacy. New York: African World Infosystems Press.

Wilson-Brewer, R. (1992). Prevention programs. In M. R. Issacs (Ed). Violence: The impact of community violence on African-American children and families. Arlington, VA: National Center for Education in Maternal and Child Health.

Wobogo, V.; Diop's 2-cradle theory and the origin of white racism. Black Books Bulletin 4, 4 (1976): 20-29, 72.

Wolff, P. H. (1973). Observations on the early development of smiling. In J. L. Stone, H. T. Smith & L. B. Murphy (Eds.), The competent infant. New York: Basic Books.

Young Black men most likely to be jailed (1990, March 10). Washington Afro-American, p. A1.

Zigler, E., Taussig, C., & Black, K. (1992). Early childhood intervention: A promising preventative for juvenile delinquency. American Psychologist, 47(8), 997-1006.

Zinn, H. (1980). A Peoples History of America. New York: Harper and Row.

ONLINE RESOURCES

Trayvon Martin

http://abcnews.go.com/US/neighborhood-watch-shooting-trayvon-martin-probe-reveals questionable/story?id=15907136#.T2QwBWJWrQI

http://www.huffingtonpost.com/2012/03/14/trayvon-martin-sanford florida_n_1345868.html

http://www.tampabay.com/news/publicsafety/crime/article1128317.ece

http://www.wesh.com/news/30692415/detail.html
http://abcnews.go.com/US/trayvon-martin-family-seeks-fbi-investigation-killing/story?id=15949879#.T2aTkZggugE
http://www.tallahassee.com/article/20120316/OPINION05/203160343/Teen-s-death-suggests-review-Stand-Your-Ground-Law needed?
http://www.aljazeera.com/indepth/opinion/2013/08/201384102857620336.html

Jordan Davis

http://www.cnn.com/2014/02/16/justice/florida-loud-music-trial/
http://www.cnn.com/2014/02/12/opinion/anderson-dunn-trial/index.html
http://www.thenation.com/blog/178370/jury-fails-reach-verdict-murder-charge-trial-michael-dunn#

Darren Manning

http://dailycaller.com/2014/01/17/cop-squeezed-kids-genitals-so-hard-he-is-now-in-a-wheel-chair-and-possibly-infertile
http://www.rawstory.com/rs/2014/01/18/philadelphia-teen-suffers-ruptured-testicle-and-hit-with-misdemeanors-during-police-patdown

Index

About the Author

Paul Tony Jackson is a clinical psychologist and bay area artivist/writer who established his teaching career at Notre Dame de Namur University and at Skyline College. He earned his Ph.D. (1997) in Clinical Psychology with an emphasis in Health and Multicultural Psychology from the California School of Professional Psychology, Berkeley-Alameda campus. As a tenured professor of psychology at Skyline College he formally coordinated and remains actively involved in the ASTEP (African-American Success through Excellence and Persistence) program. Dr. Jackson assisted in developing the ASTEP Math Academy and a handbook for the development of culturally sensitive learning communities as part of the GROWTH (Genuine Rebuilding Opportunities with Technology and Humanity) curriculum project. His therapeutic background includes working with families, couples, children, seriously mentally ill patients, troubled teens and treatment of drug addiction. He is co-author of "Psychology: Connections in Theory and Practice" 4th ed. and is co-founder of PranaMind brain training center. Growing up in one of the toughest neighborhoods in South Central Los Angeles served as a catalyst for his research in the area of Violence Prevention, which focused on bridging the gap between the psychological and sociological literature in developing an Afro-centric model for clinical treatment. Dr. Jackson is also a member of the Association of Black Psychologists.